THE TERRIBLE UNLIKELIHOOD
OF OUR BEING HERE

21ST CENTURY ESSAYS
David Lazar and Patrick Madden, Series Editors

THE TERRIBLE UNLIKELIHOOD OF OUR BEING HERE

Susanne Paola Antonetta

MAD CREEK BOOKS, AN IMPRINT OF
THE OHIO STATE UNIVERSITY PRESS
COLUMBUS

Copyright © 2021 by The Ohio State University.
All rights reserved.
Mad Creek Books, an imprint of The Ohio State University Press.

Library of Congress Cataloging-in-Publication Control Number: 2020034370

Cover design by Nathan Putens
Text design by Juliet Williams
Type set in Adobe Garamond Pro

♾ The paper used in this publication meets the minimum requirements of the American National Standard for Information Sciences—Permanence of Paper for Printed Library Materials. ANSI Z39.48-1992.

For Bruce and Jin, my heart
And for May: my spooky action at a distance

There is just as much certainty that the
Summer Land exists as that your mind exists.

—Andrew Jackson Davis

"Sometimes I prefer the dishonest truth,"
she said. "It's more interesting."

—My grandmother May, to her son-in-law Bill

CONTENTS

ACKNOWLEDGMENTS

Thank you to the journals in which some of these chapters originally appeared. Many of these publications appeared in different forms or are not used in the book in their entirety.

Brevity: "Journey's End"
Hotel Amerika: "How to Die Knowing That You'll Live Forever"
Image: "The Arrow of Time"
Slag Glass City: "Wendy"
The Lenny Letter: "Finding My Grandmother, One Psychic at a Time"
The Manifest-Station: "Bone Structure"

Thanks also to Essay Press, where "The Arrow of Time" also appeared in their digital chapbook, *Curious Atoms: A History with Physics*.

The title "Here Bullet" comes from a book of the same title by poet Brian Turner.

For this book, Donald Hoffman, Chiara Marletto, Julian Barbour, Lee Smolin, and Giulio Tononi generously offered their time and their dialogue, not to mention the gift of their ideas. Their time and help were invaluable. The errors are my own.

Chris Paola, Ralph Savarese, and Bruce Beasley read, listened, and helped shape my thinking. David Lazar has offered me more long-term support than I deserve. Great gratitude to Kristen Elias Rowley and Patrick Madden for believing in this book. Taralee Cyphers shepherded this book through production with efficiency, kindness, and care. Kristina Wheeler in her copyediting many times brought eloquence where there had been muddle.

PART I

THE SUMMER LAND

UNSTUCK

My grandmother believed she had no physical body. She had given birth to my mother who had given birth to me, so there were a lot of bodies in the story, a lot of flesh-swell, to be so nonexistent. And they had nested in each other like *Matryoshka* dolls, if you can imagine the smallest *Matryoshka* doll not simply nesting but struggling to claim the same body as the larger—dividing and dividing, just to achieve eye and limb and breath. And each body had to be unstuck from the one before on a tide of blood and fluid. The strenuousness of the body's efforts—what you could call the absurdity of the strenuousness—only made my grandmother May more convinced.

Do you believe in a God who would cause suffering and death? she would ask me, answering herself before I got a chance to. *I don't believe in a God who would cause suffering and death.*

May gave birth four times.

When my grandmother was young, she skinny-dipped every summer morning—in Barnegat Bay, an estuary, so a place where fresh and salt water meet, a bay coming off the Atlantic Ocean and flowing forty-two miles down the New Jersey coast.

I know May skinny-dipped because she told me, and so did my mother, but I heard it from the latter less often, as my mother did not think well of this. My grandmother could pass judgment with the best of them—people were *no better than they ought to be,* illegitimate folk were *born under the rose,* no human transgression existed for which my grandmother didn't have a quaint and pouncing phrase—but she loved nudity. She loved the body, and if she saw ballet on television she said of the ballerinas' bodies: *They are like art.* Or, she would add, like a poem.

My grandmother did not swim naked in my lifetime, that I know of. I was her first female grandchild, born to the eldest daughter who had finally, at age thirty-three, gotten herself married. I want to pretend I remember her nude swimming, as it captures something: her denial of the body, her worship of it, seemed struck from the same bell.

May is still a young woman in this time I'm thinking of, perhaps with an embryo inside her (she may not know it yet, that mad cell splitting, the rush of this new being to catch up to the body my grandmother could so relish and dismiss).

May wakes up in the morning at the shore and drinks her Lipton, teabag in, no sugar. The kitchen is a galley that could hold maybe two of her, slender as she is. Buckling linoleum meets the arches of her feet. She goes into the even tinier bathroom that holds a toilet and a sink (cold water), pees luxuriously (holding it in while drinking her tea, one of those small ritual denials we all practice), sluices her face. She hangs her floral nightgown on the towel rack and knots a pink chenille bathrobe around her, then crosses the dirt road. Sun inches up, a thin moon fades. Next to the bungalows a field of cattails grows to her height, and on a few, red-winged blackbirds sway. Their call holds a strange high pitch and then a click like the *tsk* of a tongue.

May stands ankle-deep in the bay that laps up to a half circle of land, a round inlet roughly the size of a high school gym. The water is brackish and laps at more cattails. No other homes nearby yet, just the two men who live in a shack at the strip of land on the other side of the water, strange men no one would listen to, so my grandmother May has only herself to make a history here.

And this is so familiar she doesn't think, just unknots the robe, drops it over the small wooden dock that holds her row-boat, and puts her not-body into the water.

WHO LOVED HER

She swims. Out to deeper water; floating. Nothing to do. The body her Christian Science teaches her has no presence—just an emanation from her mind, which with work can free it from its doomed love affair with belief in its own existence—bobs like any of the things always bobbing in this water: sea-weed the thickness of a girl's braid, a handle of a cup. A crab's yanked-off claw. Things wash in. Storms drive them from the ocean to the bay then the bay drives them to our cul-de-sac of water. When I was a child I found two baby mako sharks tossed up on the beach after a squall. Even the seas have their ends-of-the-road.

May believes in something that's weightless, a bobbing belief. Christian Science doesn't do more than give words to her conviction. Her belief needs the words only as much as her spirit-body needs its pretend flesh, so she will get out of the water and smoke a cigarette, have several manhattans or a few glasses of wine with dinner, things her religion strictly for-bids. She uses caffeine and has tried opium, which she smoked overseas.

While she lived I loved this woman, I'd have to say, in a charmed and hopeless way that probably mirrored how my mother loved her, and how my grandfather loved her. She swam, lazy circles, and floated. She didn't care who the hell loved her.

FOR ONE

I will be born and love my grandmother, and I will be like her, maybe most like her, of all her children and grandchildren. Unlike other members of the family, who reacted to her with a bit-off skepticism, I did and do rule out nothing. I have her to thank for a reflex of credulity.

And I share her fascination with the mind. As a child I thought obsessively about thinking. Thought had a physicality to me and I wanted to catch it in the act not of narrating, as it does, but of preparing to do that, coiling and forming itself. This felt different to me than absorbing its talk. I tried to look under the surface of each thought, as if I could dig that up and find the root-tangles and half-cracked corms and grubs that had fed and tended it. I imagined things with great detail and wondered if that imagining could make them true.

This focus meant disappearing a lot into my own head. My fifth grade teacher Mrs. O'Sullivan gave the boy behind me the job of poking me in the shoulder with a sharp pencil when I drifted away in class.

This mental habit didn't mean I had nothing else to worry about. I did have other things and I did worry about them. There was the cemetery across the street, uneasy with graves, the man in the apartment behind us who beat his wife; we heard the thuds, the jerky scuffling, through the walls. The man in the fedora who attacked children in my neighborhood. The way my mother looked at my brother and me sometimes, as if she wanted to cast her eyes to one side and will us away. We had a small apartment and we children were too much body for it. I would worry about things and then wonder how exactly I was worrying.

This fascination with consciousness may be why, as soon as I could, I wanted to change mine. I wasn't any Timothy Leary, an intentional psychonaut. I was a high school dropout in urban New Jersey and drugs formed part of the landscape. Still, I became a heavy user by any standards. Psychedelics mix the above layer of consciousness with the below, exposing its chaos. Heroin slows down thinking and lets you hold a thought till you've exhausted it. Drugs, in their own way, are questions.

I used drugs long enough that when I stopped and my mind came back fully, I wasn't sure what to do with it. Televisions then were boxes studded with knobs and dials, controls you had to get up and change with your hands. My mind felt like a television with the knobs fallen off.

My grandmother was never sad for me, which I found reassuring. I never found her sad on anyone's behalf. Now I call her feral. Like a wild creature brought indoors, her domestic surroundings never seemed to take. She was a polite feral thing and I was one with a wildness you could see. In any case, I was not sad for me either.

ARS POETICA

My fascination with the mind didn't end when I quit putting altering substances into mine. I still need to know how it works. I wonder what in the world, given the nature of quantum reality, can be said to be real at all, a question that would have fascinated my grandmother, in a more wholly metaphysical way.

I have come to think of myself more as a questioner than a writer. My grandmother bequeathed me questions about the nature of consciousness, about reality. I wanted to see who—neuroscientists, physicists, even psychics—might have answers. Though *answer* turns out to be the wrong word.

Scientists use the term fallibilism, "the idea," as put to me by physicist Chiara Marletto, "that it is important to make mistakes as fast as possible for knowledge to be created fast." The mistakes I believe are questions too, and I want to be a fallibilist. Though I don't want to give all my answers over to the possibility of fallibilism. I also want my grandmother's certainty.

I think death, like the death of my mother four years ago, ups the question ante. As did the death of my grandmother two decades ago. Something sticks fast in us after such a disassembling; the person grows in some ways, with that final punctuation making her more of a complete statement. Then we struggle to read it.

But I gain a certain satisfaction just in posing the questions. That they can be asked implies something—maybe limits, maybe a temporary philosophy to fold around this whole confusing business.

I often feel as I prepare to do interviews that the most profound stories lie in the questions, in the urgency they have now, the fact that the edge of science now cuts toward things like whether we can say consciousness is a sham and we exist like zombies; whether the world we know is the world that exists; whether time is an illusion; whether infinite versions of ourselves live in infinite other universes. Or that consciousness, rather than nothing, is everything. And that for many questions, clear and reproducible math or experiments exist that support the conclusions.

I asked Julian Barbour, a physicist and a giant in time theory, what he wanted people to take away from his theory that time has no reality—there are just an endless series of Nows that exist like Polaroids laid out on a table, all together.

"Life is often difficult," Julian told me. "I hope the layperson will get happiness and interest from the realization that we are all part of some huge marvelous process." I don't have this reaction myself, but the possibility is interesting.

I also wonder how much, in science, we go with our gut beliefs, our own patterns of thinking. Said Julian to me, "I have always enjoyed life, instant by instant." What if you only loved endings, like mystery books, where ripping out the last two or three pages would nullify the whole. What would you believe.

ARS POETICA II

My mother, when she read, preferred mysteries, and she read authors like Agatha Christie and Erle Stanley Gardner, books with one opening question and a solution. The death happens in time and the consciousness of the murderer gets unspooled by the detective. If the detective is Hercule Poirot, his own habits of thinking—the "little gray cells on which one must rely"—will be part of the story too. None of these forces in the book is problematic, though thought now is an enormous problem in science.

My mother left these paperbacks lying around when she finished them, unruly from her habit of turning pages with a licked finger. I picked them up and read many, especially in middle school. I learned that after reading thirty or forty of these books (and they read so quickly, you get to this number in no time), you can tell, ten or so pages in, who the murderer will be. The recognition has something to do with the facts of the crime, but more with intuiting the relationship the author needs to maintain with the reader. The murderer won't be a point-of-view character, or have a strong motive, or no alibi. The answer can't be obvious or alienating. And the author can't pull a murderer out of nowhere at the end. The person must have presence in the story.

You learn to recognize those characters who have just enough narrative identity, who are neutral enough, with a sound but not airtight alibi, who seem to have no motive. The person who is un-obvious but not unthinkable. The inconspic-uous killer. There's only one such person in every book.

Why can't you write a book like this? my mother used to ask me, showing me her mysteries.

I told her honestly that I would turn it into a complete mess. I would give things away.

RESEMBLANCES

My grandmother, like my mother, was small, with hair the shade of the tea left in her china cup, thin brown over fair. Her face—wide-nosed with a mouth always lightly curving, well cheek-boned—bore a resemblance to the face of her great familiar, the cat. Her eyes the blue of the veins now pushing out of my hands, and once out of hers: de-oxygenated blue. As far back as I can remember, she had a curve to her back that bent her over slightly, the so-called dowager's hump, marking a family history of early osteoporosis. On her though, the curve looked fitting: It accentuated the way she seemed oriented to some other dimension. She was a comma of a woman, always holding in, always marking the place where things paused.

It didn't occur to me till after my mother's death, going through photographs, that in many ways she and her mother looked alike. They shared a face shape, thin lips, and hair. Both about five feet tall, my mother prettier. My mother's eye shape was deep and came from her father, and she had a sharper, narrower nose. But a resemblance existed, which the eye discarded because they were so utterly different.

My brother and I emerged into the world looking like my father, with his dark hair and southern Mediterranean, part Turkish, features. My mother would look at us and wail, "What happened to *my* genes?"

IMMORTAL TRUTH

My grandmother spoke to spirits. Given her beliefs, she spoke to them as one spirit to another—a message passing between two like beings in different planes of existence, coded and implicative, like a lover's text—and it's true she was chummy almost, in her table-rapping sessions with Simon, the spirit she contacted, in her Ouija-ing. She read tea leaves, which I don't believe she was terribly serious about, and held séances, which she was. She performed séances at home in Westfield, in northern New Jersey, but most loved to do them at the shore, during her and her children's summers there. May enjoyed life moment-by-moment but was no Barbourite. The future was a real thing and she wanted to possess it.

May believed that she could control and change the world with her mind. This was, in its way, a practical belief, meaning that it had no base in psychology—no sense that the world is what you make it, or it's up to you to decide how you feel about things. These truths my grandmother might also have acknowledged, but they skirted the central one: If the matter of the world had only spiritual reality and poured forth from your mind, you could make it do anything you wanted. "Spirit is immortal Truth; matter is mortal error." So says the Christian Science creed.

And death only moves you from one spiritual existence to another, from the summer land you built beside an estuary off the coast of New Jersey (a heavily polluted estuary, but still, a potent symbol) to a place called—by America's First Prophet and Clairvoyant, Andrew Jackson Davis—the Summer Land.

SPIRITS

My grandmother spoke to spirits, and that would be a reason she'd talk to me even at times when my consciousness was such that normal speech had fled. My grandmother saw me wandering through her Summer Land, stupefied, sometimes passing out. I weighed nothing in those years, tall and barely over a hundred pounds. It especially showed in my pelvic area—my hipbones cliffed around a sunken sea. I dropped out of high school. My grandmother would talk to me as if things were normal. Though I'd inserted a barrier between the raves going on inside my head and what was outside of it. She understood the divorce between speech and the mind.

MORTAL ERROR

My grandmother had four children, in this order: Mary, Mildred, Edwin, Kathleen. She had her children between 1920, the year of my mother's birth, and 1929, Kathleen's. These children were physical and had bodies as well as minds, bodies that, like my mother's, would hurl themselves—tantrum-y, splotch-faced and breath-holding to collapse—onto the floor. My grandmother never quite got over this.

Edwin was named for her brother, Edwin Radford, a writer and journalist. Edwin Radford and his wife Mona together wrote mystery novels and he also cowrote an advice column called "The Old Codgers" for the London *Daily Mirror.* He wrote one screenplay, for a B movie, a noirish movie titled *The Six Men.* Kathleen was a nod to the name of my grandmother's sister Katherine, who died young in a motorcycle accident.

My mother had me and my brother Chris; Mildred had Melinda and Nerissa; Eddie had Helen, Diana and Lavinia; and Kathleen had Mark: eight cousins. Three of us would develop a psychotic condition—bipolar disorder or manic depression. My grandmother would never learn this, which didn't matter, as she didn't believe it existed. I have a son, Jin, twenty-one now, but he won't appear here much; he is wonderful but not part of this story. He has no foot in the Summer Land.

The siblings' spouses respectively were my father Nick, my Uncle Bill, my Aunt Catherine, and my Uncle Joe. My Aunt Catherine called my father, Joe, and herself the *outlaws.* She felt my grandmother treated all of them except Bill badly. She complained about this to me and Helen.

STAKES

1. That a hurricane destroyed the Summer Land, actually a hurricane that was part cyclone and part nor'easter, a Frankenstorm, as meteorologists say, the kind of thing that happens with global warming, as freak (or once freak) temperatures layer together. Though the hurricane had the name of a kindly waitress in a New Jersey diner, Sandy. I can picture her, gnawing the eraser end of her pencil. *What would you like? Nothing? I can do that, Hon.* One bungalow (the larger bungalow) cast down drunkenly, bending the knee. The other licked away. Almost whole, too, quadriform, staggering in the water. The buildings that served as my body's body, in a way my other home never could.
2. That May died, and then my mother. Though she did not believe in death but could never articulate what she thought would happen in place of it.
3. That time bends, as Einstein proved, like the gum I used to chew, Double Bubble. I had a gross inability to keep gum inside my mouth. Either I blew huge bubbles or ribboned it out around a finger (my finger being gravity). There's that thrill when it thins just to the point of tearing. Maybe God feels this, or the universe feels it, with bending time. Maybe not.
4. That the consciousness May revered so much is still pretty inexplicable in technical terms—how it forms, why and how it talks to itself.
5. That, in the subatomic universe, things—quanta—can exist in multiple states at once, a quality called *superposition*. There are various ways to interpret this.

6. That quanta can also be entangled, meaning they can connect in special ways with one or two other particles and change each instantaneously, even across the universe.

7. That basically for subatomic particles none of the rules apply: They exist without clear position in space, in time. At which fact we may want to say, "Who cares, they're not *us*," but that's false: They make up our atoms, our molecules, our gizzards and brains and skin, and are more us than *us*, given that the pronoun *us* is just a concept bouncing around in our heads somewhere. From our perspective quanta behave like a gang of unpredictable drunks spinning chaos in the basement of the stately mansion. Though the drunks are the true beings, and the manners and mores of the upstairs people, an elaborate pretense.

8. That one of our greatest physicists, John Archibald Wheeler, said, "Useful as it is under everyday circumstances to say that the world exists 'out there,' independent of us, that view can no longer be upheld."

9. That John Wheeler believes awareness changes the past as well as the present.

10. That my grandmother preceded John Wheeler.

11. That physicist Andrei Linde believes the problem of consciousness is almost wholly unexamined.

12. That my grandmother preceded Andrei Linde.

13. That many physicists believe reality as we perceive it doesn't exist at all, but is really mathematical formulae, or computer simulation, or some reverberation of consciousness itself.

14. That another scientist I spoke to, theoretical physicist Lee Smolin, believes that the fundamental universe, including gravity and space-time, are emerging forces, not fixed ones, and they evolve as we evolve. "Time," Lee told me, "is the least illusory thing we know."

15. That another theory holds that reality is infinitely more complex than what we see. This view compares our perceptions to the icons on a computer screen, each a simple, small, geometric image, shorthands for terribly complex files that may have hundreds of pages or photos or Excel spreadsheets. Cognitive scientist Donald Hoffman created this analogy, of the icons. Fitness for survival, he says, increases the less complexly we see the world.

16. That neuroscientist Guilio Tononi told me of his theories of consciousness and how it exists outside the brain, and said, "Language is not good enough to explain this." Then he said, "Each of us exists much more than the damn universe that we see." He calls his measurement of consciousness *phi*.

17. That I am far more superstitious than my grandmother.

18. That *no phenomenon exists unless it is observed, yet even when it is observed, its state is unpredictably determined by the act of observation* is something my grandmother would say, though it was actually said by physicist John Barrow.

19. That May's beliefs keep looping back to me and seeming true, or closer to true than most people get, in spite of the fact that they're false.

20. In another physics theory called constructor theory, we stop asking what predictions we can make based on testable theories and predictions based on laws of motion and initial conditions and the like. (As in considering the conditions of our bungalows, the shoddy building, the poor foundations, at the time of Sandy.) Instead, says constructor theorist Chiara Marletto, we ask, "What are the transformations that can be made to happen?" Her first name means *clarity*.

21. That, trying not to believe in psychics, I consulted psychics until I found one who had insights I couldn't explain, then

I stopped. Perhaps there are many things I don't want to know, or not for certain.

22. That a structure built not to last lasted for more than seventy years, then split with a shock, as at that point you think a thing will last forever.
23. That destruction can be, in a weird way, a relief.

ENTANGLED

My cousin Helen and I, two years apart, were a unit, close in ways that bothered our parents, though not because I was a bad influence. Our closeness and their concern came long before I could be called that. As a twosome we were mouthy and we did everything together, even peeing. Together we argued raucously against the war in Vietnam. We taught our younger cousins to curse, and had them sing rude songs we memorized from Monty Python. My Aunt Mildred hollered that we were *saucy* and we found that hilarious, and our scoffs I suppose made us count as even saucier.

Helen as an adult goes by her real first name, Olivia, but none of us called her that. I guess my aunt, a Greek immigrant who was born on the island of Samos, had not totally sold my Uncle Eddie on that name. He called my cousin Olive Oyl during the time my aunt insisted on using Olivia. It infuriated my aunt but rather than trying to stop him she changed the name used for her daughter to her middle name, Helen.

CHATTEL HOUSE

My grandfather and a Bajan nephew built May the two bungalows, or the two cottages—we always called them one of these two words—down at the shore. My grandfather Louis descended from Red Legs, poor white men of Barbados arriving in the 1600s on that island as lifetime indentures, shipped off from Ireland and England for criminality, or rebellion, or being poor.

Men of the lowest classes could be indentured by being snatched off the street. My grandfather said at least one of my ancestors was taken as punishment for his part in the Monmouth Rebellion against a king suspected of Catholicism (Monmouth rebels who weren't peasants were hanged).

These men who were "Barbados'd," as they also called it, were captive for life and could be sold and resold, often for bags of sugar. As a book titled *A True and Exact History of Barbados,* published in 1657, close to the year my ancestors made it to the island, put it, "This island [Barbados] is the Dunghill whereon England doth cast forth its rubbish . . . manured the best of any Island in the Indies." My grandfather always said an ancestor was a Monmouth rebel, and he had a Monmouth-y hatred of Catholics all his life. These lifetime indentures did the scut work of the island until the African slave trade began, then they rose to become a privileged racial class, though Bajan wealth—mostly from rum and sugar—went to absentee landowners until well into the twentieth century.

For a long time, Red Legs were the lowest class on the island; they were also called Baccras, because they were only allowed to sit in the back rows of churches. When I went to the island as a young woman the relatives I met were middle class and worked with their hands: A cousin's husband painted houses; his mother-in-law catered, making—it seemed—mostly pineapple-upside-down cakes and patty melts. (She, Elizabeth, and her daughter drove us around the island, Elizabeth jumbling her granddaughter loose in her lap in spite of the spiky roads, cooing to the girl in her Bajan accent, *See de sea, see? See de sea, see?*).

My grandfather's immediate family lost what money they had, according to my grandmother, through gambling. My grandfather told us a family member—I believe his uncle—was a rum runner, a criminal who stole rum by smashing ships on rocks, using a lighthouse-shaped false light.

What my grandfather built my grandmother resembled two versions of the Barbados chattel house, a structure created to house tenant laborers on plantations. Wood planks stacked into a thin-walled enclosure, a steep roof (as we had on our Big Bungalow), a house just large enough for a couple of small rooms, and the whole thing on cement blocks. Our Little Bungalow was even smaller, two rooms and a little bathroom on a cement foundation you could just park a car on. Its only divergence from the chattel house was its flat roof, which my cousins and I climbed onto most nights via a wooden ladder.

Chattel houses were designed to be built in a few weeks and be movable. Many chattel houses were built after the Emancipation of 1831 by former slaves, who were stuck to the same land as before, throwing up a two-room shack to live in and moving it when given the order to move.

That my grandfather built chattel houses for his wife and his children is an irony I suspect was not lost on him. Though "chattel," meaning movable property, referred not to the houses' dwellers (as *chattel* once referred to slaves) but to the houses themselves. I imagine Louis relishing the joke, putting his family back into the kind of dwelling his forebears fought fiercely to escape, attaching to him—as if they had no choice—the wife who constantly left him to travel, and the four children he left to her, or to their own devices.

I believe my grandfather always had a mordant humor, and that he laughed within his mind fully as much as he failed to laugh outside of it.

PERSON DETAILS FOR
MAY LOUISE RADFORD

My grandmother May was born in King's Lynn, Norfolk, in 1895, but grew up in the village of Sutton St. James in Lincolnshire, on the west coast of England. Her father had been a small shopkeeper who also ran the tiny post office. May immigrated to the United States from nearby Mildenhall, where her family had moved.

Mildenhall was a US–UK air force town in which May probably began her nursing career, though as it went on she no longer believed in the reality of the bodies she made her living tending, as so many of them over the last few years (including my grandfather) became the war-wounded: the faces drawn back from eyehole and nosehole and the flesh scarred into bark by mustard gas; the many blown-off limbs and digits, flesh-shreds and stubs of bone, including, again, my grandfather's, short a finger from a sniper's bullet. The near-corpses she turned every day—meat on a spit, no one who did this could resist the comparison—to minimize the bedsores. All a thought, vanquishable.

May sopped blood from, sponged out, and covered with gauze hundreds of very bad ideas.

I wonder if at this time my grandmother fell in love with her naked body. Real or unreal, its wholeness must have felt luxurious. Two arms, two legs, ten fingers, ten toes! I imagine her going over them as she lay in her bath, with as much love as any parent admiring a newborn. An awe at the completeness of the thing, in one case because it comes from nothing, in the other because it's so easy to return it to the nothing again.

My grandfather, her patient, offered May a ring. I suppose he had recovered and they'd dated, in whatever way people did in postwar, post–Edwardian England. She took the diamond and soon told her mother she did not want to marry Louis after all.

My great-grandmother said that no daughter of hers would take a man's ring and not marry him, an episode my grandmother described to me matter-of-factly when I was in middle school. She did not seem emotional about it one way or another though she very much wanted me to know, as she also around this time wanted me to know she found my mother chilly and never understood her. My mother never cried, she added, when my grandmother told her that her first fiancé, Angelo-Andrew, had been killed in the Second World War. I think this reaction reflected less my mother's grief, which was lifelong and genuine, than her guardedness toward her mother. She never let her mother see her weak.

My grandmother accepted her mother's command to marry. I think it suited her to go, and I think it also suited her to say she hadn't wanted to. She was a young woman at the time, the second child from the top in a family of six. Her family called her *Girlie.* Though when she sailed from the country of her birth at age twenty-four, my grandmother left Girlie behind to develop May. My great-grandmother cried at her leaving despite causing it to come about, May told me.

I suspect my grandmother wanted to go to the US and Louis proved a handy way to get here. My grandfather was a bitter man and saw life as futile—and worse, ridiculous—but I think it may have taken my grandmother a while to realize his bitterness wasn't complex or interesting, and it didn't have the power to change into something else over time.

In spite of that bitterness her new husband wanted to have children, a strategy I think for trying to postpone or push forward what he saw as a human life's pointlessness. Perhaps one of his children could change the terms of the argument. And what would that look like? For a child to have a child? For a child to cure cancer? Either way it comes back to human life: making it, preserving it. If it doesn't matter, it doesn't matter.

Maybe when May realized she couldn't think her way out of this dilemma on his behalf she realized she'd truly married in error. Or not: My antisocial grandfather gave her an enormous amount of freedom. She herself solved the problem of life's meaning with what she summed up for me as her "metaphysics." My grandfather, a materialist and an atheist in most ways—though he had a very West Indian tolerance for spirits—never did.

My grandfather Louis had been a UK citizen (through his Barbados birth) and then a Canadian citizen, but was Canadian at the time my grandmother nursed him. Why he and his mother were in Canada, and why he changed his citizenship, is a mystery.

My grandfather's war records don't solve many of the mysteries. He fought from the ages of twenty-five to twenty-eight. At age twenty-one he had had gonorrhea, which my brother and I decided probably came from visiting brothels when he worked at a lumber camp. He would have been treated then with an element like iodine or mercury.

His records constantly refer to my grandfather's amputated finger as "the stump." Apparently, the stump didn't heal well. During his second round at the front, which my grandfather volunteered himself for, he was shot in the neck, a bullet that stayed in his neck for life. A medical note said he could feel it when swallowing.

After the war my grandfather headed from England back to Canada and then down into New York. I'm not sure why these were his movements either. My grandmother followed him, sailing in 1919 on a ship called the Royal George. She arrived at Ellis Island on August 26 of that year. Eleven months later, in July, she gave birth to her first child, my mother Mary.

WASPS

"Oh, your Uncle Bill can come to the lunch table in his undershirt," my Aunt Catherine says, spreading mayonnaise on white toast. One of her insistences at the shore is bacon, lettuce, and tomato sandwiches. I don't like them but we often eat this way, one thing per meal. On weekends we have crullers and jelly donuts from a bakery down the road in Bayville, and many phone calls fly around to see who's picking up the *buns,* as we call them, on their way to the cottages. In spite of the generic term, if you picked up anything but crullers and jelly donuts, there'd be trouble.

"When your father does it, it's 'Nick, I guess someone's bringing down the level of the party.'" My grandmother does in fact say this.

Helen and I are my aunt's sounding boards. She says, "I'll tell you what I said, I said, 'May, the party's pretty informal already, isn't it?'"

My father complains about my grandmother too. He and my aunt accuse her of "only liking the WASPS." It will be a while before I realize this means White Anglo-Saxon Protestants, not flying insects. My father and Uncle Joe come from Catholic families, Italian and Irish American, respectively; my aunt, born on the island of Samos in Greece, was Orthodox. My father and my Uncle Joe come from poverty; my uncle's family were immigrant coal miners, pretty much all of whom had died from black lung by the time I came along. My uncle escaped the mines by running away from home at sixteen and joining the merchant marines. Because of his merchant marine time, he loves to sail, and buys and rehabs wooden boats. My father too grew up poor, his father only educated through the fourth grade, and often out of work. Only my Uncle Bill's a WASP.

My aunt smiles to herself and stubs another scorched and lipsticked butt into the ashtray. She chain-smokes and drinks astonishing amounts of coffee, brewing pot after pot. She has a tall stainless steel electric coffee pot and it and she are rarely apart. We wash out her cans of Maxwell House and use them for gathering things. My aunt is the only woman in the family who wears lipstick and keeps her nails polished. My mother generally regards these practices as a vanity. My grandmother does not consider useful any habit that isn't portable.

Helen and I are putting the tomato and lettuce on top of the bacon. In a minute we'll be asked to call everyone to the table, set with old flatware and paper plates.

"The party's *pret*-ty informal," my aunt repeats, mostly to herself.

A STELLAR KEY TO THE SUMMER LAND

The Summer Land is the afterlife of most Wiccans and pagans, as well as spiritualists, and a concept my grandmother would have intimately known. There are as many Summer Lands as there are individual movements, but all of them share an allegiance to the earthly, a coastal paradise approach to the hereafter. The Summer Land is like here, but with picking and choosing. The Summer Land isn't quite material and isn't quite immaterial. People there exist in bodies, but those bodies are luminous, "flaming emanations" coming from the tips of the fingers. Andrew Jackson Davis, the nineteenth-century "prophet of Poughkeepsie," visited the Summer Land through astral travel and carefully drew and mapped it. Much of this work is contained in his book *A Stellar Key to the Summer Land*, published in 1867. It is built, he wrote, of atomic emanations arising from humans on the earth. Our shedding, and its growing and building, feels at least somewhat physical.

Davis's thinking forms the root of most American spiritualist churches and he's still influential in that world. I don't know how many followers would go along with the paradise formed of cast-offs from the human body.

Davis's finding of the Summer Land formed a high point of his prophetic career and he wrote about the place in many books, also illustrated with his drawings. His most important Summer Land work, *A Stellar Key*, was published in 1867 Davis calls the existence of the Summer Land a "certainty" in light of the order of the stars in the night sky, describes it as a "stratified belt of matter," and draws it as a cloud of bushes under an arch, that arch thin and white, a child's cut, curved paper. The great sun covering the universe that Davis draws elsewhere looks like an end-to-end slinky.

In the Summer Land you exist in time and out of time, in the logic of a place that can be pointed out on a celestial map, yet where you stay and defy the rules of matter. You live forever. It's the shore and my grandmother at the shore, time not as flexed arrow moving forward but time that squeezes, distorts, moves back: the Einsteinian time discovered in my grandmother's girlhood, though few non-scientists understood it then. Einstein discovered time gets warped by gravity, like the liquid-y candy stretched into taffy by machines at Seaside Heights, or my gum. Maybe the sweetness of the afterlife comes from time's warping.

So the Summer Land partakes of the material but hosts what does no longer. If you want to swim there, you swim. If you want to eat, you eat. Summer Landers who are compatible form Associations, just as men like Davis did in Davis's time (the prophet was born in 1826). If you want a glass of nectar in the Summer Land, you can have it, and besides a glass of wine I can see a glass of this cupped in my grandmother's trim fingers. She would want specifically the nectar of the honeysuckles that grew thick around the bungalows. Whatever you do in the Summer Land, you escape that past world of age and gristle and blood and become smaller and lighter. Again and again Davis calls what we do when we die and arrive in the Summer Land *living*.

IN THE SUMMER LAND

Often my teenaged body and I moved through the world as I imagine my grandmother's body did, in view of her beliefs. That is, me and my matter found a physical equilibrium in which the body loses existence and becomes theoretical. Once at a concert in Asbury Park I was full of quaaludes and heroin and stumbled outside, alone, halfway through. I don't remember the leaving or know why I did. Outside I collapsed on the pavement; it's hard to explain, the state of not being conscious or unconscious either. When I came to myself, the concert had ended, the world was dark, and several cops were yanking on my arms. My ride had left. Somehow the cops decided to leave me alone and somehow I found another ride.

What matters here is the sensation, and the sequence. I left the theater without knowledge of my body, which meant it crashed around doing its own unpredictable thing. As my eyes opened and the yanking began, it returned, a weight that reinstated itself around the nerve endings finding themselves scraped by sidewalk. It had been gone and come back, in the manner of physicist John Wheeler's comment that the only phenomena that can be said to exist in the universe are observed phenomena.

GIRLS

My body-illusion got born in 1956. My grandmother had had only grandsons before me—my cousin Mark and my brother—and given the Radfords' tendency to produce girls she must have felt smug about that. No doubt she made much of it to her sisters when they called each other, which they did not do very often. The Radford sisters always had a one-uppish relationship. When my grandmother mentioned to one of them that she was cooking spaghetti, her sister responded, "May. We don't eat *paste*."

After me came five more girls, each one of us evidence of a physical world that could not necessarily be shaped. For someone who didn't believe in the reality of the body, my grandmother cared an awful lot about what genitals came attached to it. She favored her son Edwin and after him, her daughter Millie. Among her granddaughters she preferred Melinda, the "sweetest," she said, and the only one of us children who'd get invited to sleep over at her home. My grandmother had no problem being clear about her favorites. She particularly didn't care for her oldest daughter, my mother.

It didn't occur to me then to wonder why she would tell me of all people her secrets, in a matter-of-fact tone that implied I would want to know or I should know, I'm not sure which. I was always and by far the most in trouble of all her grandchildren, not even close to her favorite, but she confided in me about aspects of her life she didn't tell anyone else. I learned early to write down what she told me and not to tell my mother or my father, who came to think I invented our conversations.

"She didn't try not to marry *Pop*," my mother snapped, when I told her about my grandmother wanting to return the ring. "That's ridiculous."

"Did she love him?"

I asked this during our second or third try at having this conversation, after my grandfather's death. I didn't realize then how badly I would want to pursue my grandmother one day (or how, like matter leading to antimatter, she'd lead me back to my mother) but I was trying. My grandfather died in his sleep, at eighty-eight, after mowing his lawn that afternoon.

I'm sure he did other things too, but that fact—the lawn mowing—was the one the family mentioned when we talked about it. He was to turn out of all of us, in spite of how unhappily he lived (or because of it), the only one to have a good death.

The death came as a shock—my grandfather had nothing wrong with him other than being eighty-eight—but my grandmother never cried or seemed the least bit surprised. She was pretty jolly, in fact, and when we stopped over afterward she'd pull out the large moonshine-y jug of premixed manhattans my grandfather always had on hand, and pour. *Louie would want us to drink this up,* she said, over and over, a far more definite reading of my grandfather's desires than she'd ever had in his life. She even insisted on giving him a Christian Science funeral (which my grandfather had made her promise not to do) and held the service immediately, before her son Eddie could make it home from a trip to Argentina.

"Well, I don't know," my mother said in response to my question about her mother's love for her father. "But I'm sure she wanted to marry him."

I asked her how she knew.

"Well, because she did marry him," said my mother. She was annoyed with me. It was very like her family to have trouble questioning things: You either came from the camp that insisted things simply were the way they were, or the camp that turned its back on reality and said they simply weren't. There was nothing in between.

7,000,000,000,000,000,000,000,000,000

You might want to know that your body consists of seven octillion atoms (if you believe in its existence), a number I hate to type because that many zeros makes me feel vaguely faint. Atoms are conglomerate particles, though humans until the twentieth century didn't know this; the Greek word we use for atoms means "uncut." Electrons orbit the atom's nucleus and in this form are unbound quantum particles. They are not stuck to anything. Quarks make up the protons and neutrons in the nucleus and these too are quantum particles. Atoms are vastly empty, so if you wanted to compress yourself into just mass, you'd be a speck of dust. Atoms have electrical charges and repulse one another.

Most of us go to school, see models of the atom that look like little solar systems, imagine these crushing together to make us. In fact, my grandmother was closer to grasping what the body is—almost nothing—but still she got it wrong. You're not exactly nonexistent or exactly existent.

Quanta exist in superposition—existing across different possible states at once—unless detected. When they come out of superposition they're said to *decohere,* and when that happens they no longer behave as unruly possibilities but as particles, subject to the rules the rest of us cosmic working stiffs have to follow. Their wave function collapses.

Electrons are, in the charming words of physics, collections of probabilities, or possibilities. If this sounds nonsensical, I promise that, though I'll return to the subject, it's not because I'm explaining it badly. It *is* nonsensical, to most of our ways of thinking. That outer electron layer of the atomic solar system isn't a ball or even a ring. It's a blur of different possibilities around the nucleus.

Your stuck-together body may not be an illusion, but you are a temporary premise that violates the logic of everything surrounding it, in the manner of a car blasting backward down a road in order to make a turn. You can get away with it quickly and in a small space, but overall that's not how things are done. And all of what's true of your body is also true of your brain— the emptiness, the almost-nonbeing of its constituent parts. Somehow, if you're like me, this fact will land with a thud. We tend to imagine our brains as their own full and special entities.

Quantum bits (my word) cannot be said to exist in any definable way unless they're detected, which is a bizarre truth I'll discuss later. They're just superpositioning all over the place. They do not have a clear relationship with time, and time itself for some scientists looks like a thing that may be illusory, or else a local feature of our particular planet and material selves. There may be particular demands of our place in the cosmos that call time into existence, as the warmth of Barbados calls up its breadfruit trees.

Our bodies make demands: Time is the "turtle shell," as cloner and physics writer Robert Lanza puts it, that we agree to carry on our backs to obtain our flesh. Once we exist as composite creatures, we have things in us that can be and will be torn apart. Barbour's theory rules out time as a meaningful concept.

So I could say that my grandmother and I exist as ancestress and descendant or I could say that the reality of us is parallel and ongoing. It is possible that particles of her body and particles of mine exist in that special relationship called quantum entanglement, always following the others' moves like synchronized swimmers, and this relationship would still be true after her death. We are Julian Barbour Polaroids, always present on the table covered with scraped oilcloth at the shore. Coexistent in some way. This reasoning about our quantum relationship physicists might dismiss as "poetry" (not a compliment), but they couldn't argue with the premises of the theory, they would just dislike the conclusions.

THE SLOW LOBOTOMY

The most dealing any of us will have with electrons is through electricity, which consists of destabilized electrons stripped off their nuclei chasing around and together releasing energy. They rush along seeking new partners to balance their charge, much like a torrent of frustrated speed daters. Their possibilities, like those daters', have force, which enables us to flip on lights, start our cars.

The most truck I've had with electricity is having it powered through my brain. When I was fourteen and fifteen, my parents had me given shock treatment. Before the first round, I had overdosed and I was depressed. My parents worried but were also tired of my behavior, my wild and self-destructive habits. I got dosed with those drugs popular at the time, like Thorazine and Haldol, the so-called major tranquilizers, or, as they were often called in medicine, "chemical lobotomies." I took these when I had to and continued to pile on the speed and barbiturates and acid and heroin I used on my own.

Shock treatment wiped out my memory of much of those two years. I still used drugs and still hung out with kids as wild and self-destructive as myself. It's possible incidents like the concert one were post-shock, part of that confusion, on top of the drugs I was using. There were also a handful of homicides and near-homicides among young adult males in my circle. My boyfriend slept with a long knife on the wall above his bed. Most older boys in my group had at least one gun.

My knowledge of these two years comes through memory fragments, the long and detailed diaries I kept, and others telling me about it later. Though people often suggest it to me, I have not done any research into this time beyond reading my own diaries—no medical records or the like. I have chosen to honor the fragments I have as a more valid record than any I could uncover, and maybe honor the fragments that pushed through the larger erasure. At sixteen my ability to form new memories improved, even though at that time I had begun using more heroin.

I have a newspaper article I clipped from the *Spokane Spokesman-Review* titled "Shock Treatment: Past Horrors Gone with New Treatment." It states, rather remarkably, that ECT (electro-convulsive therapy) "doesn't turn people into vegetables, not if it's used intelligently." I have hung on to this article: It feels strange to be associated with a treatment described as a "past horror." And that you should IQ test your doctor, in order not to become a "vegetable." Nowadays shock is done unilaterally, with the electrodes on the side of the brain farthest from the memory centers. The current is also lower. I have no idea if this really makes it better.

Some facts about shock treatment in the 1970s: it was given more than 70 percent of the time to women; it was very lucrative; it was described as a "slower-acting lobotomy"; it was used in psych wards and psych hospitals as a means of control. When I was hospitalized at fifteen, staff used shock as a constant threat. We patients called the shock machine, which often sat in a common room, the *buzz box*.

This use of shock for punishment became the subject of congressional hearings in the 1980s. In my day, the fear and regression shock caused were considered healing by many medical people; patients would wake up nursing on those plastic bits, like infants. All these things combined to turn psychiatric thinking against it in my second year of shock. In 1975 *Psychology Today* ran an article titled "Electro-Shock Therapy: Let's Stop Blasting the Brain." This request didn't help me any.

What we know: Electro-convulsive therapy does what it sounds like it does—it causes a grand mal seizure. It has been done for almost a hundred years and we know that it can lead to, at most, a few months of relief. Early shock treatment used things like Metrazol—a form of camphor—and snake venom to cause convulsions. The "shock" of the name does not refer to electricity but to the state of shock the treatment induces. The short-term nature of the gain is usually acknowledged even by enthusiasts, who say it gives time to begin drug and talk therapies. Meta-analyses of ECT studies by researchers John Read and Richard Bentall found that ECT has no benefits over sham or placebo ECT, as long as the latter uses anesthesia, so patients actually believe they've been shocked. Other researchers found benefit; though in some studies, results are based on feedback from people other than the patient—hospital staff and the patient's family.

How ECT works, if it works, is still a guess. It may be that it resets electrical firing in the brain, or it may just be that whatever relief it gives (which doesn't happen with every patient) comes from head trauma. If a branch falls on your head one day as you walk, you'll generally have a period of confusion but also lack of affect, or emotion, that can last a while.

My brain had been blasted, a blur of electrons flying through, stripped and greedy. I think in retrospect this gave a kind of permission to consider mental absence a norm, to find violence a norm. It's hard to explain being strapped down, a bit in your mouth, conducting gel and electrodes on your temples, except that then your sense of what people can do to other bodies gets stretched. Maybe I'm just making excuses.

IMMEDIATE REPROGRAMMING

In the 1970s a doctor named H. C. Tien created a treatment he called electrolytic therapy, or ELT. ELT began with electroshock and made use of its regressive effects to reprogram patients, bringing them back to the start of their infancy, presumably erasing early trauma. Tien wrote in a medical article, "The patient is prepared [through ECT] and transferred in the infant-like state for immediate reprogramming in the family session. The patient is usually transferred on cart to a private bedroom for the family session in which the patient is actually bottle-fed by a relative, parent or spouse in order to re-establish rapport and a new consciousness with significant others in the family. . . . Most patients accept best the formula of half chocolate and half-white milk." This doctor condemned the way other patients were left "alone and confused" after shock treatment. I suppose I give him a point for this, and I remain most itched in my curiosity by that choice of milk.

ARE YOU THERE

The Holly Park of my childhood held derelict boats, gouged and half-sunk in the bay or Potter's Creek. It had always been a place in which some people lived marginally, in such a way that if you walked a mile or two you'd move out of the zone in which they operated and in which they were known. Our bay didn't offer the best swimming or the best food—other than blue-claw crabs—but it had enough if you weren't picky. The area was technically wetland, one big marsh; the lagoons criss-crossing right behind our bungalows pearled and pulsed with mosquito eggs and larvae.

My grandmother told me stories of the two men in the shack across the water who'd lived by foraging. You could eat things like crab and blowfish—which we ate ourselves, pounds of it, in the summer—and hunt food like muskrat. With muskrat you could also sell the pelt to furriers, and one childhood summer I befriended and fed a muskrat I named Mark (why I gave him the same name as my cousin I have no idea), who came crawling up to me one day in July with a bullet in his gut. He bellied himself under our house to die.

Many winters when I was young people broke into our bungalows and camped there. An aunt or uncle would discover the evidence, going down in winter to check on the houses after storms, or sometimes just when we opened up in the spring: mugs with a scurf of Nescafe, scratchy blankets out and strewn on the slept-in beds. Canned food opened and emptied. I seem to recall more than once the remains of a campfire on our linoleum floor. No one minded, including my grandfather who built the houses.

The squatting wasn't upsetting to me, but it was eerie. It reminded me of the stories my mother told me of a childhood friend named Jane, whose widowed mother had no money and had to rent a house no one would take, cheap because it was haunted. The ghosts moved the furniture around at night and the children drifted off to sleep to the sound of all the determined scraping across the floor and woke to find the house rearranged. *They got used to it, they just moved it all back,* my mother said.

We walked in to the leavings of our own ghosts.

As I grew, and more real beach houses appeared at the shore, the marginal population dwindled. I remember the characters of my childhood, though, sometimes people who seemed built out of a single, rare idea: the teenage boy whose eyes reacted to a world I couldn't see and who was obsessed with snapping turtles; he always had one he rode in the water, grasping its back flippers, or carried around tucked under his arm. Now and then for no reason he lashed it out at people's faces, no joke, as these turtles have sharp beaks and grow crazed and aggressive out of the water. Then there was the middle-aged man who rolled his entire body in the bay mud—thick, both very black and very green at once—and called himself the Mud Man. He chased children.

And there of course was us. Some people must have known about my grandmother's skinny-dipping, and my insomniac grandfather roamed at night through the dark. My grandmother who believed our bodies were things imagined and transparent. She sat with her children and asked *Are you there?* of a small table.

Simon knocked on the table or tipped it to answer questions with *yes*es and *no*s. Surely her children confided in their friends about an evening's séancing. We never asked who lived in our houses when we weren't there but my mother and her sisters asked Simon if he knew how we all would die. And I was never told his answers to that question.

STRANGE

I recall my Aunt Kathleen and my mother telling me, when I was young, a story of a neighbor, though for once it wasn't someone at the shore. He lived close to a house the family lived in for a while in Plainfield, New Jersey, on Quimby Street, by coincidence the name of one of Mary Baker Eddy's friends. It was a place that both called *out of the way.*

"He killed skunks," my aunt said of the man, in her high-pitched voice that seemed to take one or two words per sentence and crack them open: *sku-unks.* My mother added that the man nailed the skunk pelts to one side of his shack of a house, so he had three wooden walls, and one fur.

"He sold them?" I asked, and my aunt and my mother didn't know, but didn't think so; they believed he collected skins.

"He would come into our room at night," my Aunt Kathleen said. She and my mother sat at the dining table at the shore, which we sat around all day if we weren't doing anything else; there weren't that many places to sit. Probably they both drank tea. My mother drank her tea very weak, and tended to borrow someone else's teabag, dipping it a few times in her hot water.

"We could sense he was there and we woke up and there he was," my aunt said. "He would stand there staring."

I was young and couldn't imagine waking up to see a strange man, a killer of skunks, watching me as I slept. And among the many things I could have told you about my father, one was that he wouldn't let men sneak into our house to stare at my brother and me. At that age I wasn't sure why such a thing would constitute a fatal breach, but I sensed it would.

"Did you have him arrested?" I asked.

"Oh no," both my aunt and my mother said. "He was just strange."

This formula recurred, in conversations about our local Mud Man, the boy who carried a snapping turtle: *just strange.* It was a mode of being that lay outside of conventions and expectations, unpredictable, unpunishable.

NORMS

Like spiritualists with the afterlife, physicists like to create terms of engagement that make their incomprehensible world feel normal. They gravitate (pun perhaps intended) toward everyday language to paste over truly strange things. Black holes are described as *bald* or *hairy,* as if they were old men. The bald theory of black holes says that these entities can only be known by mass, momentum, and charge. *Bald* here is a metaphor for the limitation of knowability, though an odd one, as a bald head would presumably be the most knowable. Hairy black hole theory says there's more available information. Stephen Hawking's last paper before his death argued for the existence of hairy black holes.

Likewise, subatomic particles come in different types, but these are called *flavors.* Quarks and leptons have six flavors each, and the flavors of quarks include up, down, strange, and charm. The word quark itself was originally *quork,* a word coined by physicist Murray Gell-Mann, who changed it when he came across the word quark in James Joyce's *Finnegans Wake.*

Physics language embraces the simplistic and sarcastic. Astronomer Fred Hoyle used the term *big bang* in a radio broadcast and it stuck, though it sounds like it comes from a five-year-old holding a sad shred of balloon. The other official term for entanglement, *spooky action at a distance,* was coined sarcastically by Einstein, who didn't believe the property could exist. It does, and his derision became an official term. Two candidates for as-yet-unknown dark matter are WIMPS (the weak) and MACHOS (the strong). We have wormholes, though it's impossible to conceive of our universe as dirt.

It feels like more than normalizing, but hypernormalizing, what's yawningly different. It's odd to look in from the outside and see papers full of massive equations arguing about flavors or hair. Drugs resembled that; you could only stay within that otherness for so long, then you had to try to prune it down to something you'd always known, to sink the strangeness of an acid trip into watching old cartoons. Heroin addicts used the terms *sick* (not high) or *well* (high). Drug nicknames grasped for the daily, like *stuff* for heroin, or *soapers* (as we spelled it) for barbiturates, a word none of us would have known came from *soporifics,* rather than bars of Dial. Maybe we created a series of simplifying entanglements between one dull item of living and another sharp and illicit one.

FACE AS INTERFACE

Donald Hoffman, the man of the theory of our world as icons on a desktop, teaches cognitive science at University of California, Irvine. He's a cognitive scientist who works in a crossover area, one that's growing quickly and is sometimes called the field of information: It melds questions of consciousness, quantum physics, computing and other sciences, to consider many questions that for Hoffman, include the first principles of the world. Don's first field was artificial intelligence, which he studied at MIT.

We talk on the phone for a while one day. I'm struck by how much Don uses the term "portals": the world as portals that obscure what they cover up, even with your physical self. Your face in a mirror, for instance, doesn't hold your inner complexity—"You know [as you look] it's a portal," he says, "to a realm of conscious experiences that's very complicated."

Hoffman also uses the term *user interface* for our world as we experience it. Unlike Julian Barbour, whose theory of time meshes with the way he experiences life, Hoffman says his theory shocked him.

"Only when I tried to build a mathematical model of perception did I realize we are constructing everything that I see," he told me. "I had to sit down and absorb that. Is it possible that the construction isn't the truth?"

Hoffman tested his theory by, among other proofs, generating scenarios where creatures like rabbits compete for resources. Again and again, creatures with what are called *interface* perceptions—perceptions simplified to show pared-down images of survival payoffs like water—beat realistic perceptions. Survival was greater the less complexly they perceived the world.

I keep seeing the phone itself and the voice on the other end as their own portals during this conversation. If this, I wondered, is the simplified version of the world, what would the complicated one be? We can perhaps in the future get some sense of that, Don tells me.

Cosmology has been pursuing the question of whether there might be one or more fundamental forces in the universe beyond the four we've identified: electromagnetism, gravity, and the weak and strong nuclear forces. Don's vote is for consciousness as a fundamental force, and he's trying to work out a mathematical equation to explain it. He believes not only that consciousness is fundamental but that most of what we consider foundational is not—space-time and matter are all just

PART I · 39

more interfaces. He is not alone at least in considering consciousness larger than just stuff banging around in our human heads, and possibly cosmic.

ENGINEERING

I spent much of each summer at the shore, at our chattel houses; everyone in the family did. There existed some system where the parents in theory called each other to say who was coming when, and every family got to pick a week to have to themselves per summer. In practice everyone lost track and who might show up and where they'd sleep changed daily. The bungalows had no phone, which added to the chaos. People would sometimes come down with kids' friends, or in-laws. For a while my father brought his father down, my Italian grandfather, a man afraid of the surf who we nonetheless dragged to surfy beaches, where he tried to stop the waves with the palm of his hand.

All together we were the Boxill grandparents, their four children and spouses, and the four children's eight children, plus random others who came and went. And the two bungalows housed only four bedrooms, though one (used for the girls) had two sets of bunk beds.

The bungalows stood close to the water, at the end of a road I didn't learn until I had reached my fifties, and mostly quit going there, was named Main Street. We had no street number at the shore and no street signs. I never saw a mailman there, though this feels impossible: DDT trucks, yes, weekly, junk men snatching at empty cans and bottles in the trash, but no mail. I did not know the address until after Hurricane Sandy, when I saw notices of condemnation stuck into the sagging remnant of the door. We existed like that as-yet-unmasked murderer in the books—uncounted, unconsidered, with no obvious impact on the story. Or like Hoffman's simplified icon, simplified more.

On the right side of the bungalows a business called Schipano's hugged the water, white, wooden, no larger than a house. It sold bait and crab traps and had a couple of juke boxes, pinball machines, and a pool table. You could buy candy and ice cream there in addition to the bait—squid in white boxes, newspapered moss bunkers, worms. Mrs. Schipano ran the place, a woman small and middle-aged and composed of a series of rounds: arms, breasts, rolling waist. Her roundnesses sweated profusely in the summer heat.

As Mrs. Schipano scooped ice cream, sweat tended to roll down her forehead into the cones. Still, we got ice cream there from time to time. I recall her as grouchy, or maybe we just tormented her in the way we tormented the beach keeper Mrs. Duffy. Mrs. Duffy ran my cousins and me off the beach more than once, her tan dimpled legs pumping under her house dress, her arms flapping, gulls squawking overhead and her mirroring them, looking like an angry bird. The wading pool on the beach had a pipe that flowed fresh water into it and a corresponding one that let the water drain; we practiced our dam building by damming the outflow with layers of mud and rock, flooding the beach.

Across the inlet was a restaurant we went to for fried shrimp or fried clams, the Holly Park Inn. Once I ventured into ordering spaghetti with tomato sauce, and the pasta arrived gummy and smothered in ketchup. My father told me I had to eat it and then tried it and said I didn't. It was an uncharacteristic retrenchment.

The day of the moon landing in 1969 my parents marched me and Helen and my brother over to the Inn and its television, a little black and white, to watch Neil Armstrong's foot land in the soft, spongy dirt.

The boys hung out at Schipano's, playing pool and pinball. The girls only went for candy and ice cream. We had territories that way; Helen and me, and Mark and Chris, the four oldest, divvied the world up by gender. We'd go into the cattails and pick a spot to stomp out a clearing, calling these our "forts." We declared war on each other frequently, and one of the things we did during war was dig deep pits, covering them up with strewn cattails, then try to get the enemy to give chase so they'd fall in. We learned this one from coverage of the Vietnam War.

We played Capsize in the water, a few of us taking out our dinghy and the others clinging to the sides, pulling the boat down while swinging at, swatting and yanking at the occupants, until one side pitched the other out and then had to scramble in and defend the dinghy themselves. We did damage—bruises and cuts, and my specialty, deep gemmed scratches. Chris and Mark nicknamed me The Claw. Still, even having had a metal oarlock smacked into a temple during Capsize, a regular mishap, we'd cry but then ask for another game and another, until it grew not too painful but too boring. We were maybe better little Christian Scientists than we knew.

Once I brought my gerbils with me down the shore and Helen and Mark and Chris and I designed a gerbil habitat on the grounds between the bungalows. We loved engineering projects. We created a lush gerbil home, about eight feet by four feet with six-inch walls, a mud house, caves, twig forests, and hamster wheels. It had picnic areas with pine cones spread with peanut butter and seeds. I remember the place bringing tears, the gerbil future it offered, of ease and amusement and plenty. A being could be perfectly happy in there. It was a rodent Summer Land. I put my two gerbils into it and within an hour they'd disappeared forever. I found this quite the betrayal.

NIGHT-SWIM

My cousin Helen and I also skinny-dipped in Barnegat Bay. We did it at night, as late as possible, and called what we were doing *night-swimming*.

Going for a night-swim, we said, and took off from the Big Bungalow wearing our bathing suits. The Holly Park Beach consisted of a square of sand trucked in and fenced off, with wooden tarry bulkheads dividing the beach from the brackish water. You went down wooden steps and dove to avoid stepping on the seaweed on the bottom, which held crabs. It was not really a beach, in the lapping surf, hunting-for-seashells sense, and friends I brought whom I told to expect a beach in Holly Park always looked disappointed. Still you had to join and wear a badge to use the beach during the day. Our shore had the inflated language of my grandmother, as if she'd named it all, though she had not; everyone called the inlet the *yacht basin,* for instance, though it never once held anything that could pass for a yacht.

The beach held the wading pool for younger children and a small swing set. In the water a rope separated the shallow water from the deep. Being allowed to swim "past the rope" meant you'd arrived at a certain maturity. Beyond the rope lay a raft in the water and a diving board with a wooden ladder.

At night it was very dark. The one road down to our bungalows, the last habitation on it, was dirt and gravel. The handful of houses that had sprung up were far from ours, with few lights. It was the kind of darkness in which you could convince yourself anything at all existed a few feet from your face, the point where the visible world faded.

Speaking to me of the mind, Giulio Tononi used the metaphor of a person on a beach in utter darkness. "You feel there is nothing there to be able to experience," he said, "but imagine it with one little dim star. It needs to have distance from every possible location. You must allow a *here* [for the star] and all the *theres* that makes, and all the theres included in other theres." Tononi calls this experience "fantastically structural." These statements confuse me scientifically, but thrill me intuitively—yes, such richness to the subjective world. I think I felt that then.

Helen and I swam out to the raft, then took off our bathing suits in the water, throwing them onto the wood. As we swam sometimes iridescence trailed from our fingers, as it did from the wake of my uncle's boat at night. The iridescence—actually bioluminescence—came from a bacteria called *vibrio.* It could look like aquamarine pinpoints in the water or twist in lines like cursive letters, and as you combed the water with your fingers to try to touch it, it disappeared and then gleamed back elsewhere.

Blue flies and mosquitoes stung brutally at night so we kept as much as possible of our bodies in the water when swimming, which was nicer anyway: the warm water insisting against every inch of us, the sense that both water and land were endless due to the dark. We stayed all the way under as long as we could, until the lack of oxygen began to burn.

When we'd had enough night-swimming we grabbed our suits from the raft and thrashed back into them in the water.

LOOSED

I don't recall ever thinking about the fact that my grandmother swam nude too; maybe the words kept them apart, *night-swimming, skinny-dipping.* I never thought about it, all the related bodies naked in that water—the former nesting dolls— how May had no doubt once menstruated potential aunts and uncles (and with them, cousins) into that bay as we had no doubt loosed her great-grandchildren into it as well. Had any of us kids been conceived in there? It was always a kind of sex: the brine, the seaweed, the crabs and fish and the eggs they bubbled out.

COUSINS

What happened in those beds in which the grownups slept double? That was how cousins got made: the four stairstepped girls who followed us; Melinda who worried and got my grandmother's love. Diana with the huge glasses who my uncle trained to recite Rudyard Kipling. (At eight she could recite all of "Gunga Din," spitting out "belted you and flayed you" with a slight lisp and her eyes focused and near panicked under those glasses.) Then Nerissa who was pretty and who I constantly let fall from the rotten steps leading into the water, and then Lavinia, the petted youngest.

HER BELIEFS

I know that my grandmother lost her faith in medicine and came to a Christian Science-y way of thinking during World War I and her nursing. I don't know if May joined the church in England, or rather as a twenty-four-year-old bride in the US. It's an American religion and the latter is more likely, but it had arrived in England by then. Besides the Bible, its doctrine comes from Mary Baker Eddy's book *Science and Health with Key to the Scriptures.* Christian Science teaches that God, the great Mother-Father, is all good, and that sin, disease, and even death are an elaborate illusion. These come from lack of faith or lack of knowledge of that God. The mind is real, the material world including the body is not. Healing is done by prayer designed to realign the patient with the true nature of

PART I · 45

reality. It is a useful religion to have if you marry a man who carries the gene for bipolar disorder.

There is no medicine in this religion, and the need to contact a practitioner when you feel your health slipping—though practitioners just help you to realize your illusion and pray your way out of it—leads to a language rich in indirection. You do not say things like, *I am sick,* or *I am dying,* though you might be lying in the road with the giant wheel of a truck flattening you out of existence. You say things like:

There is a belief regarding myself and a truck.

Apparently there is a belief about myself and a truck and it may involve dying.

Apparently I am dying.

OUTSIDE THE CONCERT HALL

Apparently I consist of weighted pieces, rasped by sidewalk. I am waking up. There is a belief about my fixed location on this planet.

I am in a suspended place, not quite living, a place of un-memory: The next day, as per usual among my friends, my good time will be evidenced by my inability to remember it. This result happened even before shock treatment, though the latter cast a new light on oblivion.

Once I was driving around with a boy I don't remember in a car full of other kids when the car suddenly ground to a halt. There were five of us and our bodies came back in a juddering pour when the car jerked them back into us. It took a few minutes, again, arms and legs weighted into being, discovering the damp plastic seats, noses filled with a hot rubber stench. One of us got out, or leaned out, and I did too, and saw that we had hit a tree, a large oak, and not just hit it but remained smashed into it, oblivious. We had for at least ten minutes been grinding into wood, too high to detect that we weren't on the road and driving anymore. Our eyes had left.

Apparently there is a tree, we said. *Apparently there is a question about the car and its existence and the engine and even our own survival.*

We were fine, it turned out, and the car, banged up, still drove. It happened according to constructor theory: the result not through the start of the car or the trajectory, just one transformation of all the possible transformations.

MIND

"God is mind," my grandma tells me. She tends a dented pot spitting jam. Wild strawberry. I found and picked the berries and I hulled them for her.

"When you don't have enough pectin in the fruit," she says, slicing green apple into the pot. (Years later I remember this and use apple to set my jam, and I even try to mimic the way she cuts apple—with one hand, casually, knife toward thumb—but I do in fact stab myself). The jam foams up bright pink and smells like a heaven in which you die on a pile of mashed fruit. But it's thin. A rainy year; watery berries; apple for pectin. May acknowledges the properties of matter when it comes to food. She calls the bright pink foam surfacing in the jam the *scum* and spoons it off. I find it highly lickable.

"The divine mind is love and it is your mind too," she says, then, "Stir this for me and keep your hands away."

My mother adds from the next room that hot jam could *pull off the skin.*

My grandmother ignores her. In a smaller pot she's melting paraffin, the square cake spreading round and translucent as it heats. Her Ball jars line up. "Your mother," she tells me. "A cautious one." My grandmother laughs to herself. I move the spoon, starting to leave a track through the thickening jam.

"Isn't it beautiful?" my grandma says. "Doesn't it smell beautiful? If we take care to understand the beauty in the world."

"*Mom,*" says my mother.

SATELLITE

I loved the things my grandma said about God and Mind and Jesus the Scientist; I spiraled around her to listen. It made me uneasy that I couldn't make literal or emotional sense of her musings. I loved her code, but I couldn't crack it.

And May wasn't grandmotherly in the conventional sense, not affectionate except in the odd verbal gesture. "My dear, how is your lady mother," she would ask as I arrived down the shore. Only my grandmother's daughters warranted the designation "lady mothers." Sometimes the granddaughters got the title "pretty pretties." Could I ever evolve from a pretty pretty into a lady mother? I have no idea, but I doubt it. And I know I'm not especially pretty.

May played favorites and could be, in her graceful way, very caustic. But I've never known anyone who so fully inhabited her own life. She did what she wanted to do and there was no question that it was the right thing, always. If she'd smacked herself into a tree, she would continue to believe she'd meant to, or that it hadn't happened. She used the word *must* often, and unlike when I used it or my mother used it, it worked: we must-ed. We drove her to and from airports and the Christian Science Reading Room and the immigration office where, once a year, she'd have her green card renewed. Though she railed about US politics she refused to become a citizen. My Uncle Bill called her *Brit,* for Brittania.

She was one of those people who serve as inspiration and repudiation, because you want to be large like that, but know you never can be. Her presence filled the room; she outdid everyone in sheer substance, in spite of her beliefs about her body. I adored her, but secretly, because it seemed foolish: to love someone who shimmered like a full cup with herself.

PULLING OFF THE SKIN

My grandmother kept up a chaffing irony with my mother, one designed to remind my mother of her mother's superior inner and outer strength. My mother was reserved, fearful, arms held close to her body, a literal reminder of the way she held things in. She seemed as much smaller than her five-foot height as my grandmother seemed larger than hers.

My mother Mary disliked children, had a pharaoh's regard for the cat, and worked when she worked doing bookkeeping. She was more of an Eddyite than her mother, running her life along the narrow track of self-denial, always when she talked laying out to others what she didn't do: eat garlic or spicy food, talk baby talk to her children, drink more than one glass of wine (and only a painfully bad white zinfandel with ice cubes), watch movies, party, dance, have female friends, paint her fingernails, believe in things. She called herself *agnostic* in terms of religion but held that attitude toward many things in her life. She always wore the same clothing size, an 8 petite, and showed a lifelong suspicion around food; she prided herself on her thinness and would note a fresh ounce on everyone else. She read biographies and her mysteries, but no other fiction.

My mother held things in until they burst out of her. She had angers but about what and how they might show was anyone's guess. Once, my father tells me, he asked her over and over if he should take a job that would mean being away, and she said nothing; then one day flung an armload of lamb chops onto the sidewalk on a crowded street in New York, yelling *No.*

Bruce, if he wishes to mimic my mother, imitates her gruff voice saying *She has a plate in her head.* She said this and many things similar, because my mother packed into her daily rhetoric all the flourishes of weird she excised from her life. Not that she did this on purpose, but somehow there seemed to be a cosmic balance involved. Whatever question you might put to her often drew the strangest fact you could imagine, delivered without self-consciousness. The plate in the head response, for instance, answered the question of whether she liked this woman, a coworker. A question about why she came home late one day became the story of another coworker leaving early to be photographed with her husband's corpse, as identification, which it turned out mattered because he'd been a wise guy with the mafia. All of this delivered in short, bored spurts while she sighed over the vegetable bin.

When my mother reached her nineties she responded to questions about how she felt with *I just don't feel very peppy.* She seemed genuinely surprised by this.

My mother petted our cats and slipped them raw chicken in the kitchen, but when she talked to them, as she did all day, she had none of my grandmother's cat-cooing but just threats. "It's beating day!" she'd announce to them cheerfully. "Today's the day for beating the bubbies!" using her nickname for cats. Or she'd pick up a cleaver and say she was about to cut their tails off. The hardest I've ever seen her laugh was at a *Monty Python* sketch about cannibalism.

JUST STRANGE

When I became as a young teenager feral and ungovernable, nothing much changed in the family. You could have called me a philosophical zombie. I lived and acted repetitively but without thinking. I dropped out of high school and put anything any way into my body. I did this at home and at the shore, while my parents fretted a little and did less. Friends in low-scraping cars or motorcycles pulled up at the shore cottages that had no address, took me away and brought me back wrecked, at all hours of the night. Sometimes I passed out on the couch. The family, my parents included, Helen says, stepped around me and did their ordinary things. As if, in her words, I was a strange kind of pet.

This was who I was headed toward being, picking wild strawberries and finding ticks in my hair (touch a hot matchstick to it or the head will stay in, my aunts taught me), playing Capsize, damming the baby pool, and cleaning crabs. We kids all did these things but three of us would end up with psychosis, five would not. Probably the three most fearful, most sensitive, but whether that's cause or effect, who knows. Only one of the three of us crazy ones spun out as I did back then, though oddly enough, when older, I will be the one to survive the longest.

WANDERING

One of my Aunt Kathleen's earliest memories was of crying on the front steps of her house in Westfield, because my grandmother had disappeared again. May turned her home into a boarding house during the Great Depression to earn what the family needed to survive, and a census from 1930 lists her boarders: George Abercrombie, Hugo Wiesenthal, Ralph Christensen, and my favorite, Leo Pottle. Young men in their twenties my grandmother had to take care of and feed. May tended to be either gone or busy. My grandfather sold insurance policies for Prudential, often going door to door. He made money during the Depression, but not enough.

And my grandmother traveled. Lack of money didn't stop her; she took any form of passage she could get, and stayed anywhere she could afford—even, on a solo trip to Amsterdam, rented a room in the red-light district. I asked her once what it was like to stay in a brothel and she said, "But the walls were so terribly thin," in that tone she had that rose at the end of the thought, as if it were partly a question. Perhaps it was; could just a shade more wall have made the all-night sex bearable, or should she have minded more that the walls were so terribly thin? Probably she should have.

We would learn from time to time that she wandered around our part of New Jersey, too, and charmed and conned people. My Uncle Eddie once stopped at a Christmas tree seller's in Fanwood, and the woman mentioned the "lovely old lady" with the English accent who stopped in admiring her trees but complained that she had no money. "I gave her a fifty-dollar wreath," the tree seller confided, at which my uncle said, "That's my mother," and paid the woman back. When we visited my grandmother, she showed us things people had given her: everything from books to cat toys to jars of jam.

My grandmother was a happy colonialist, never judgmental about any place or any people, but never doubting the right of her own kind to be there. She did not bring much home from her trips, aside from the occasional photo—my seventy-nine-year-old grandmother in front of a Kenyan sunflower, or posing with a Maasai warrior. She was not a woman who tended to acquire much. She had no masks or carvings or more low-brow souvenirs, spoons with place names in the bowls or Eiffel Tower handles, that sort of thing. When she was home there was no evidence she ever left, and when she left there was little evidence she'd been there.

HER WORLD

It is hard to overstate the importance, in the nineteenth and early twentieth centuries, of otherworldly movements. At its late nineteenth-century peak, spiritualism had eight million adherents in Europe and the US. There were thousands of straight-up spiritualist churches and groups, whose focus was on communicating with what went vaguely by the term "the beyond"—spirits and the dead. There were personality-driven groups, like Madame Helena Blavatsky's Theosophy, a mashup of Eastern and Western mysticisms that laid the foundations for our New Age. Blavatsky was a Russian who changed her citizenship to the US but spent much of her adulthood in India. She looked grim with pale, surprising eyes, swaddled in cowls and enormous coats in every photo I've seen of her, like a prescient grumpy toddler. For many women, spiritualism opened a way out of poverty, or just, as in Blavatsky's case, middle-class or upper-class boredom. In all of that—under, on top of, sideways from—lay belief.

Groups like the Hermetic Order of the Golden Dawn moved toward applied magic, spells and so on, while still conducting astral travel and séances. Séances became such a popular form of entertainment that, reading accounts of them, it's not clear how deep a role belief played, versus ennui and a desire not to play one more hand of bridge. Even Queen Victoria conducted séances, speaking with her dead consort Albert (and she did believe in them), as did several of her prime ministers, Gladstone and Disraeli.

You could choose not to believe in the chatty dead in this time period, but you couldn't ignore them. A lawyer in the British television series set in this era, *Rumpole and the Dear Departed,* says, "What I can't accept about spiritualism is the idea of millions of dead people (there must be standing-room only on the Other Side) kept hanging about just waiting to be sent for by some old girl with a Ouija board in a Brighton boarding house, or a couple of table-tappers in Tring, for the sake of some inane conversation about the Blueness of the Infinite. I mean at least when you're dead you'll surely be spared such tedious social occasions." Truly, for those who'd been silenced for so long, the nineteenth-century dead proved dull or, at least, lacking in much intimate knowledge of death. Mediums tended to go on about spirit halls and the dimensions of the people who live on Venus, or they'd tell stories of who they were in previous lives. Florence Cook, a very popular Victorian medium, claimed to have been the daughter of a buccaneer.

Many people, like the poet William Butler Yeats, drifted from one spiritualist group to another. And the Society for Psychical Research formed both to test the validity of other group's claims and to do its own experiments in phenomena, like contacting the dead. The group wasn't just skeptical, but expected to find scientific proof of the paranormal, woven among the frauds. It attracted members like Arthur Conan Doyle and William James. Each spiritualist group tended to create its own cosmology, many strangely complicated, with levels and rings. Theosophists go at death to a place called Kama-Loka, where they stay until they can break away from their sensuality and move to a self-created heaven, Devachan—a term borrowed, very loosely, from Tibetan Buddhism. Most groups had some version of the Summer Land.

And I should note many of these groups still exist, though they are now much smaller.

This is the world my grandmother came into. Florence Cook died and remained a controversial figure—condemned as a fraud by some, though once vindicated by a renowned skeptic with the apt name of Crookes—when my grandmother was ten. Theosophy peaked in the early twentieth century, while she grew into her womanhood. She would have seen posters and bills for psychics passing through town, newspaper articles about them, local gossip. Not just the usual *Do you know what so-and-so said about so-and-so?* but *Do you know what dead so-and-so said about so-and-so?*

William Butler Yeats and William James and the great turn-of-the-century thinkers conducted psychic experiments, spoke to the dead, or at least considered the likelihood of so speaking. I imagine my grandmother's family, the Radfords, did as well. No one of that generation remains to ask; the children of my mother's cousins don't know. In any case, no one of this period could ignore spiritualism, any more than our children can ignore self help, or going gluten free, or juicing. It would have been natural for her family to try to speak to her dead sister, Katherine. It may well be that séances began with her as a pastime, as they were for many of her peers. But at the time I knew her, May named houses, quoted truths, embedded in the earthly paradise she created for herself the influence of her spirits.

All this spiritualist debate occurred in the public eye, in the same period that saw Einstein's theories of special relativity (1905); general relativity (1915), which established that gravity affects space-time; and the discovery of subatomic quanta (1900). Few spiritualists pointed to these as proofs of their hidden and bendable worlds, though they could have.

THE PROPHET OF POUGHKEEPSIE

Andrew Jackson Davis was a hirsute man whose head hair flowed backward and beard hair flowed forward, his face a solemnity between two tressed waterfalls. His hair was dead black in youth, dead white in age. Davis, born in New York state, received his name from a drunk neighbor who loved President Andrew Jackson. The boy was called just Jackson. He had a bumped nose that resembled my father's (and mine too), and tiny round glasses. He is listed on many spiritualist churches' websites as their prophet. He's called the "Poughkeepsie Seer," or the "John the Baptist of Spiritualism," though it's unclear to me who that makes Jesus. A newspaper article about him, in his day, called him the "spiritualist Galileo."

Davis had his first clairvoyant experience at the age of twelve, hearing a voice telling him to have his family move to Poughkeepsie. He persuaded his father to do this, though the move meant financial ruin for the Davises, and death for his mother. She became ill from the dank miasmic basement where they had to live. Davis chronicles these events in his memoir *The Magic Staff*, though he does not question his visions.

In Poughkeepsie, at seventeen, Davis discovered that when hypnotized by a mesmerist, as hypnotists were called, he became clairvoyant (the hypnotic state was called "the magnetic sleep"). He could diagnose illnesses, read the pages of books that appeared before him, and astral travel—zip around through a spiritual projection of his body. He flew on and over the earth, seeing animals and rocks in their lit up, spiritual state. He would go on to wing the universe, touching down on other planets and other realms, including, frequently, the Summer Land.

In one journey Davis received a magic staff from the spirit of the healer Galen. At that time Davis became a psychic healer, seeing organs inside the people who came to him as if their skins were "transparent as a sheet of glass." He saw energies dimmed around diseased organs. He derived treatments from the magic staff—which had lists of diseases and their cures—and from his visions. These could be odd and less than ethereal: Davis had one deaf man sleep with warm rat skins draped over his ears. For another deaf man, he recommended oil extracted from the boiled hindquarters of precisely thirty-two weasels.

The beliefs of Davis's that have most endured come from his trance writings on the nature of the afterlife and the nature of the universe. His vision of the Summer Land lives on in many New Age spiritualities. Another metaphysical insight, the law of attraction, launched our US positive thinking movement. It claims that attraction is the fundamental law of the universe, holding bodies and planets together, and that mental positivity creates good outcomes through attraction.

Davis described the universe as a mental emanation of a force he called the Great Positive Mind or Great Positive Power, a kind of God: the ultimate attractor. All that exists is mental emanation, including from the human mind, and the human mind can be awakened to participate in the Great Positive Mind and reach the "superior" state Davis found in trance.

Davis communicated with spirits but he did not conduct séances, always working in his trances, which he learned to self-induce. He cautioned in his writings and public lectures that not all spirits were good, and that spirits needed to be kept in the role of teachers, not masters. He tried in all things to be the voice of reason: He preached the need for a "sensible communion between the peoples of Earth and their relatives in the Summer Land." He did not approve of the contemporary craze for séances with physical manifestations, like goopy ectoplasms and scrawls on slates. I don't know what he would have thought of my grandmother's Simon.

Davis most directly dismissed mediumship in his 1870 book *The Fountain: With Jets of New Meaning,* and the response from the spiritualist community was furious, spurned. One spiritualist newspaper (of which there were a surprising number) called him a "castaway." Davis wanted his visions to be understood as coming only from clairvoyance, not from raising spirits. And so, this article's author wrote, "the wailing in the angel-world is consequently loud, and in the Summer Land their phantom teeth are heard to gnash," in despair at Davis's apostasy. I love the latter phrase so much I have to repeat it: "Phantom teeth are heard to gnash," though "gnash" comes from the Old Norse and means teeth grinding noisily against one another, and "heard" would imply noise even without this etymology. It's one of those charming examples of spiritualists' obliviousness to the lines they themselves drew between the physical and the ethereal.

THE UNIVERCOELUM

Andrew Jackson Davis's primary spiritual master was Emanuel Swedenborg, the Swedish mystic whose writings were translated into English in the mid-1800s. Swedenborg, too, astral-traveled through the universe and to other spiritual realms. He became one of Davis's spirit guides.

Davis had many thousands of followers, a surprising number of them doctors, and an even more surprising number clergy. An early and ardent follower of his was the Reverend George Bush, distantly related to our presidents of that name. The Reverend Bush dropped his support when Davis admitted he didn't believe Jesus was divine.

Davis's astral flights taught him about the machinations and workings of the universe. The "univercoelum," as he called it, sprang from a great "ocean of fire" that had no particles because it was all the particle there was. It formed a "vortex of infinity." Contemporary Davis followers see this as a vision of the big bang.

Davis had in his insights, much like his spiritualist critics, a paradoxical relationship with matter. There is a split between the material particularity of his visions, and the insubstantiality of it all, a meat-ghost split he seems confused about. His description of the Summer Land comes off so detailed and chirpy it reads like an ad for an American subdivision: the "splendid scenery," "the lovely groves and vines and flowers which infinitely diversify the landscape."

Davis provided precise numbers and qualities for all that he saw: the 800 million tons of atomic emanations that rise each year from human bodies to become the physical realities—plants and rooms and water—in the Summer Land. The distance of the spirit-world from our planet, 103 billion miles. The spirits in the sky, who live in a pastel glow. At death a ribbon rises from the area of the heart, turns into a steam-cloud three feet above the chest, then becomes an inverted pyramid in which a "spiritual germ cell" births the ethereal body.

Davis also charted the heavens. He declared the reality of the then-speculated-upon planet Neptune, and identified a ninth planet past it, which turned out to be Pluto. His admirers seize on these accuracies, too, though Davis also believed humankind came along six thousand years ago. And that most of our solar system's planets housed sentient life. The people of Saturn, he noted, were particularly advanced. His description of those Saturnlings gives a glimpse of his sensible spiritualism: They have a deep sense of right and justice, live in spiritual communion, have large heads, and are very symmetrical.

Davis considered himself both metaphysician and scientist, as did his followers. His scribe and acolyte William Fishbough described Davis's work as outlining "the structure and laws of the whole material and spiritual Universe," and Davis was rarely talked about in any positive way without use of the word "scientific."

Given his drive to theorize on what holds small particles together, the fallible nature of time, and where and how the whole mess that is this universe began, we could call Andrew Jackson Davis a physicist, perhaps not an accurate one, but certainly as hungry for answers as a Julian Barbour or a John Wheeler. If hunger is measured by scholarly output, Davis had more. They had their instruments and their math; Davis had visions.

Throughout his books, Davis declared his visions and theories provable and physically true. Part of the reason for the thousands of pages he generated is simply that: his endlessly long and convoluted rationales.

Davis's books have gone through many editions and he still has followers in the US and England. He was known well enough in his time to be mocked by Edgar Allen Poe, who stuck a character based on Davis in one of his short stories, a character named "Martin Van Buren Mavis, sometimes called the 'Toughkeepsie Seer.'"

Davis drew what he saw in his astral travels, and in his visions on earth. He made pen-and-ink sketches, sometimes drawing normal landscapes with one otherworldly detail: stretched spirits enclosed in what look like tears above a hill and valley; a circle in the sky with black holes and a ray streaming out of each one that looks exactly like my showerhead. Actually, I realize as I keep looking, the holes are meant to be teeny spirits.

BRUCE AND ME IN SUMMERLAND, KNOWN AS THE SUMMER LAND

It never occurred to me that if I really tried, I wouldn't find my grandmother. My mother, no; she was so slight a woman. But my grandmother, with her metaphysics, her voice that touched down on consonants so delicately, and rose at the end of a thought. Her voice must be out there, reachable. I began a series of trips and psychic visits to find her. Many were less than memorable: the reading that predicted I would travel again and again to North Korea. The obvious cold reading I found most of the time, a method where psychics throw out vague hints ("I see a person and the letter M") reading your face, to see if they're striking a chord, then refining their guesses as they watch you.

Bruce and I found Jade the medium visiting the town of Summerland (one of many Summerlands in the world, and pronounced *Summer-lind,* heavy accent on the first syllable) in southern California. We had just dropped our son off at college. We drove through Summerland and then back down through Santa Barbara, the coast of which has a series of old snags covered with nests, nests high and on every branch, making the snags look like nest candelabra. Clinging to each nest a cormorant, head alert at the water.

Cormorants will build their nests out of anything. They'll use the bones and fragments of dead birds, including other cormorants. An egg may hatch and a fledgling grow on the torn and rotten wing of a father or grandparent. They are birds of use and reuse.

Summerland, California, is a small town founded by a spiritualist named H. L. Williams, "to make," as he put it in a letter, "Summerland what it was intended by the spirit world." To this end he bought a large ranch named Rancho Ortega and divided it into twenty-five-dollar lots, which he sold to other spiritualists, though he seems to have had a soft touch and to have given many away. Williams held spirit gatherings where hundreds of white tents of camping spiritualists vee-d up across his property. He built a hall, unofficially called Spook Hall by locals (including those who used it), for community séances. Many mediums traveled or even moved to Summerland, including Harry Allen, a man who could only summon up spirits when he was very drunk. The spirits he called appeared as drunk as he, and often drunkenly thrashed onlookers to the point of breaking bones.

Allen's story gives a strange perspective on the spirits we call: how they imbibe something of your body, drunk if you're drunk, I'm not sure what, but something, if you're hungry or grieving. Our Simon drew from my grandmother's body, salted and incorruptible as it was.

The first family of Summerland eventually converted, like my grandmother, to Christian Science. Local historian Rod Lathim writes that conversion was "difficult" for the many family members who were born psychic, as they "were still psychic and retained their double sight or sixth sense." Lathim also worked as a young man at the Becker family home, the so-called Big Yellow House, when it was a restaurant, and he reports playing in the wine cellar with a young spirit he named Hector, and also seeing the second floor of the house "so filled with entities that I felt as if I was in the midst of a party. . . . Women in flowing gowns and men in black tuxes danced and drank." It sounds striking until I realize how close it is to a scene from *The Shining*.

The spiritualist goals of Summerland got sidelined by the land's natural oil and gas. The money to be made brought people not of the kind Williams, or his spirit world, envisioned.

But as Bruce and I drove around Summerland we saw tarot cards in windows, maps to haunted places in a grocery store. Williams' vision didn't seem entirely lost.

As we sat on the deck of our rental—one small room called a "treehouse," emerging from a stand of incense cedars—we drank wine and watched the yard next door. It had palm trees and old furniture grouped into seating areas between them, even a mattress or two laid out, with tucked, thin Indian cottons. In that yard a middle-aged surfer guy with dyed hair was teaching a young boy how to clean a bong, using soap and bleach. This was half a decade before weed legalization.

"You have to get all traces of the weed out," the blond man tells the boy. He lectures with gravity in spite of wearing just a sag of swimsuit and regards the boy with a parental look that means, *I doubt you are taking me seriously enough.* Are they flying somewhere with their bongs? The father seems to feel the bong-stakes are high. The boy has red hair, probably a hint to the older man's original color, and he looks neat and preppy, hair cut like a newscaster's. He's perhaps twelve. He listens to his father's formula of 10 percent bleach to water, plenty of suds, with a dutiful look, but not one that suggests he necessarily craves this knowledge. Though he handles the bong familiarly. Surely the two have shared it more than once.

My grandmother is more of a cormorant than she is a bong guy; she gathered in, she did not teach. While she may have shared her beliefs with me, she did it without any sense that I'd understand them. Her small private smile always signaled the opposite. She loved to talk and I was willing enough to listen and pull things out here and there. I feel how I have grown upon and into the tatters of her feathers. I realize how little I have told my own son of her, because I still have little sense of what I'd think of as the overarching story.

TEACHING

The spiritualist church founded in Summerland still exists. It's moved five miles away, to Santa Barbara, and it's called the Spiritualist Church of the Comforter. It follows the teachings of Andrew Jackson Davis; their website lists him as our country's "First American Prophet and Clairvoyant" and contains links to his writings. Every Wednesday, the church holds a "message service," when the spirits, for a small fee, answer your questions.

The Church of the Comforter has sunflowers everywhere: sunflowers cast into the stones at the entrance, sunflower paintings, handpieced sunflower quilts. Live sunflowers, drooping and a little wilted, in a vase at the altar.

The sunflower, clocking its head toward the light, is spiritualism's symbol.

The well-dressed, sixty-ish, blond woman who meets us at the door has a spiel she's been repeating to visitors (of whom there are only half a dozen, including us): "It's one question for ten, two for thirteen, three for fifteen dollars, and it's not *her* who answers the questions, it's the spirits talking through her. And she can't ask particular spirits, just the ones that are around." She jerks her head toward the altar where the *her*—the medium, also the church's pastor, Jade—waits.

When the woman finishes I ask her about a painting I've been eyeing on the opposite wall: It looks like a portrait of Andrew Jackson Davis.

"I think it's him," she says. "But what's really interesting about that painting is, the spirits painted it. They do that. We put a sheet over the canvas and pick it up after three hours, and there's a painting there."

She says this as if it's a regular thing, though the painting has an odd muted quality, a style that resembles no other paintings in the church (I will encounter this again at spiritualist places—spiritualists call them *precipitated paintings*). I suppose all spirits could paint differently. Though I suspect the thick-oiled sunflower paintings came from terrestrial hands.

Bruce and I each pay for the three questions, and the woman hands us an envelope with three index cards and a number on the outside. We are to write our questions on the index cards and wait for our number to be called. I'm "2."

I hear voices murmuring behind the altar. Presumably "1," a young woman judging by her voice, has already been granted her audience. I hear the medium use the word *pregnant*, some whispering, and then the medium's voice saying one could be pregnant with an intention or an idea.

Bruce has been reading the church's website. He's fallen hard for the way the church refers to death as "so-called death," as in one of their core principles: "We affirm that communication with the so-called dead is a fact, scientifically proven by the phenomena of Spiritualism." He has repeated "so-called death" over and over and tried to reenact one of the spiritual-ists' funerals. We imagine the not-dead dead dropping in, the whole service in air quotes.

I am amused by their many references to "science." I can see how Christian Science won some of these folks over.

Jade is also blond and about the age of the woman at the door. They resemble each other, though Jade's wearing brighter clothing, and she looks both more perky and more watchful, alert to our hands and faces. My three questions concern my mother's death, my grandmother's presence in my life, and whether I will ever finish or publish this book.

Jade takes my questions from the envelope, reads them quickly, and squinches her eyes while she hugs the flowy fabric around her knees. My mother, I learn, was in a hospital at the end of her life, and is sorry for what her death put me through. My grandmother wants me to write about spiritualism and will speak to me through automatic writing.

"Your grandmother is very excited about this book," Jade tells me. "She thinks it's the right time for the story of spirit communication to be told."

Jade leans forward, smiling. She seems fond of the idea herself.

I leave the church feeling a little hope about the accuracy of the answers, which Bruce quashes by pointing out how guess-able they were. He's right; given my age, that my mother would have to do with a hospital at her death was a no-brainer, and how could the death of an elderly parent not put you through a lot?

Bruce, when his turn came, asked about something that had happened to his father when his father was three, a deeply traumatic thing his parents wouldn't talk about. Whatever the something was, his father blamed it for his becoming a violent alcoholic.

"Tell me what happened," Bruce says some version of.

"I can't. You don't know what happened," Jade says, "because your father doesn't want you to know. He wants to protect you."

And that was that. We pass the candelabra-ed trees back to our treehouse, and see the boy who's finished his job cleaning bongs.

A SHEET OF GLASS

Andrew Jackson Davis called Jesus a great moral teacher, but not of God in the Christian sense. Other than this, it's hard to miss the similarities between his teachings and those of Mary Baker Eddy's Christian Science, which came after him. Davis's universe, like Eddy's, was immaterial. In both, our mental attitudes change our reality. Both write protracted arguments for why their theories are science.

In spite of his early devotion to rat skin and weasel butt, Davis would go on to dismiss most disease as the result of wrong thinking, or "mental captivity" to beliefs outside the Natural Law of the universe, as Davis defines it. It is a lack of right thinking and spiritual equilibrium.

Whether Davis directly influenced Mary Baker Eddy depends on who you believe. Some historians feel Davis had a strong influence on Christian Science thought, which influenced an admirer of both Davis and Eddy, Phineas Quimby. At the very least, Quimby, a hypnotist who put Davis in trances for a while, adopted Davis's theories about the supremacy of the mind and material immateriality, and passed them along to his close friend Eddy. Whether she adapted them, or they just concorded with her beliefs, who knows. Often Davis and Eddy are impossible to tell apart. Davis calls his universal power "the Great, Positive, Omnipotent Mind." Eddy describes hers by saying that "all is Mind, and its infinite manifestation." "[The human] Mind is the Master," Davis writes, "of all beneath" the angelic realms.

As Davis said, "When the mind is agitated by fear of receiving any disease, that moment the body is susceptible," so Eddy wrote disease "is fear made manifest on the body."

META-SHAME

I imagine that my mother, raised Christian Scientist and part of that religion until her marriage, found her own mind terrifying. Christian Science is only good news if you feel that your mind is under your control, and she did not feel anything was under her control. She would have had both shame (at her illnesses, her depressions, which she would never name but were palpable) and meta-shame. A true Eddyite would have no reason for shame and no shame itself, a feeling that must have, if you follow the logic of the faith, ramifications for the world. As would any negative feelings, if your mind is part of the mind of God which is synonymous with the universe, however you work out this relationship.

THE ORIGIN AND PHILOSOPHY OF MANIA

In *A Stellar Key*, Andrew Jackson Davis mentions, almost as an aside, that people in the Summer Land can kill themselves. "Friendly and sympathetic spirits" will be present and will try to stop them, he writes, or, if unsuccessful, guide them on their "darkened passage" to another realm. This takes me aback.

In another one of his books, one of many books of his with an enormous title (*Mental Disorders; Or, Diseases of the Brain and Nerves, Developing the Origin and Philosophy of Mania,*

Insanity, and Crime, with Full Directions for their Treatment and Cure) Davis calls electricity the "maddening spirit" of his age. He blames it for most cases of insanity. This also grabs my attention—its reversed entanglement with my own electricity "treatment"—but it turns out he blames the presence of electric lights for ending natural sleep.

Davis lists many other things as causes of madness: ill-treatment, too much phosphorus, masturbation, over-excitement, poor "germlines," even the brain itself. It is a dual organ, he writes, and a man may be haunted to madness by himself, hearing himself inside rave and scream. One voice seems to be always shut inside the brain, heard only by the other. In one man's case, his second voice argued blisteringly with every opinion he expressed. The man's response was that he found this voice "humiliating."

Most of Davis's treatment recommendations involve kindness, which I appreciate. Davis also recommends, for greater mental health, more contact between the people on earth and those in the Summer Land, which brings me back to point one: the suicides. Which influences go which way? Unclear.

ANGELS AND DEMONS

There is in Geneva, Switzerland, a place called CERN in which a seventeen-mile-long tube called the Large Hadron Collider froths with protons, frothing in opposite directions at very high speeds. They complete each round of the tube in one ten-thousandth of a second. They speed clockwise and counterclockwise so they'll collide, releasing neutrinos and other particles, the smashes telling us things about how particles behave and come to be. The LHC gave us the closest look we've had into what the big bang might have looked like: recreating through collision the first soup of particles.

The Large Hadron Collider weighs almost ninety thousand tons (the weight of a large aircraft carrier) and lies underground; it would crush a topside structure. There are other devices and accelerators at CERN, but when scientists talk about the place, most often they talk about the LHC.

Bruce and I arranged a CERN visit but we cannot see the actual collider, as its electromagnetism would strip out our credit cards, bombard us with cancerous rays, and, if we had pacemakers, stop our hearts. Loading regular people into the lead suits it takes to survive down there would be a lot to ask, though I wrote to CERN in advance, citing us as a form of "the media," and they've graciously provided a physicist to answer our questions for a few hours.

CERN stands for *Conseil Européen pour la Recherche Nucléaire,* which translates as European Organization for Nuclear Research, though CERN results go instantly to physicists everywhere.

Rolf Landua, the physicist whom Bruce and I have at our disposal, explains this by saying CERN is "an infrastructure, like a bakery—we produce the croissants, but they're eaten by scientists around the world."

Rolf's hair starts in force toward the back of his head, with a spry patch vee-ing forward across the top. He has blunt but jolly features and looks German, which he is. His field is antimatter, or the lack of it. Like many other things—dark matter and dark energy—antimatter is a universal element we cannot find enough of. Antimatter and matter should be roughly equivalent in our universe, both spit out in equal amounts at the big bang (which would result in both matters self-canceling and not much of a universe being left), but in fact it's rare. There are theories, but no one knows why.

Rolf is very pleasant and good at explaining himself, though much of what he says flies past us: how they measure all events with energetic protons, blips on readouts.

In response to large questions, such as one I pose on what may have existed before the big bang, Rolf says some version of, *Well, this universe is the only "observable consequence" we have to study.* He likes this phrase, "observable consequence." After a few of these questions about what may exist outside of what we can measure, what may be implied, he says, "It's like you are asking to describe a big beautiful house that has burned down. There's nothing there to tell you."

Rolf sighs at times like these, as when I ask him about the fine-tuned universe, the fact that the cosmic forces allowing life-forms like us to develop are unlikely, as unlikely as a jet plane destroyed by high winds being put back together by those same winds, all while still in the air (in the words of physicist Michio Kaku). It's sometimes called the Goldilocks universe or Goldilocks enigma. Fine-tuning can imply severely good luck; a multiverse in which everything that can be exists; or, a theory Kaku floats, an "unimaginably advanced" civilization controlling the constants of our universe. The order of the universe is hard to consider without acknowledging what could look like intention, at least without the multiverse.

At this line of questioning, Rolf not only sighs but blows air out of his mouth. I don't get the sense he's irritated at me for bringing up the question, but at the cosmos for allowing it to occur. I also detect a stance I'll find with other physicists at CERN: You stick to what you can know and sidestep what you can't. I don't find this a scientific choice, but a human one.

And in spite of Rolf's croissants, when it comes to our cosmos, he rejects metaphor.

"You can't use metaphor in describing the universe," he tells me, when I've asked a question I forgot to log in my short-hand notes. "You can't say it's like a billiard ball, that it's like anything."

Bruce and I understand that this statement is not about metaphor but about the universe: It is irreducible, it is not *like* anything. We are writers and to us, this is a hard saying—the universe is not only inconceivably strange but also inconceivably itself. Its strangeness lends itself, as Landua says, to "too much speculation" and I can see how that's true: infinite mind, slinky belts. Theosophy's Devachan. Mellow and symmetrical people living on rings.

OBSERVABLE CONSEQUENCES

Probably the single biggest achievement of the Large Hadron Collider is the discovery in 2012 of the particle called the Higgs boson, the so-called God particle. The Higgs is a key part of the process that allows mass to have mass. Peter Higgs predicted its existence in 1964, but finding the Higgs proved elusive. And desirable—we material bodies are all indebted to the Higgs.

Smithsonian magazine called the discovery of the Higgs the "most important experimental achievement" of the last fifty years and it's hard to argue with that, but I don't get much sense of that at CERN. Landua tells us that the Higgs appeared as a "blip on top of the statistical readout." That feels anticlimactic, a minor thing emerging from the crowd.

"How did finding the Higgs feel after so long?" I ask him.

His jolly face collapses into another sigh. He understands I wish to hear a story of seeking and of triumph.

"Actually, we are disappointed when our theories prove true," he says finally. "There was maybe fifty-fifty excitement about finding the Higgs. Our mindset is that we want to find what we don't know about and haven't predicted."

Landua's greatest source of visible pride, it turns out, is having helped the filming of the movie *Angels & Demons,* based on a Dan Brown novel. The film opens with scenes at CERN, and

Landua guided around actors like Tom Hanks. It's a tangible achievement, and probably lends itself safely to metaphors.

I could understand this attitude about the Higgs if they hadn't nicknamed it the *God particle*. Though what can it do but usher us into materiality? I expect for Andrew Jackson Davis, and Mary Baker Eddy, and May Boxill, the discovery would be a nothing, a misdirection, a yawn. They had already found what scientists don't know and haven't predicted.

AT THE SUMMER LAND

Andrew Jackson Davis says of the Summer Land's residents, rather vaguely given his intimate knowledge of the place, "It is not easy to tell why, but the dwellers are gregarious." Contemporary Wiccans and Pagans revived the idea of the Summer Land. Wiccans describe it as a lovely green place that's "less dense" than the earth. You can age in it, some think, but you will age more slowly than you do on our planet.

My grandmother, like many spiritualists, mostly didn't communicate with the dead when she held séances, but with spirits whose job description consisted of being spirits—they exist all around us, etheric souls who live on other planes of existence but have strangely ordinary names. At death I'm sure my grandmother would have expected to meet souls she already knew. I picture her in the Summer Land confidently calling out names, as she might down at the shore, striding by the cattails but not looking in any particular direction, not entirely certain who was there but figuring that in all the *Marks!* and the *Eddies!* and the *Marys!* and the *Mildreds!* somebody familiar would emerge.

And what would she think of the gregarious Wiccans and Pagans and others sharing her after-place? She would have little sympathy for Wiccans who believe in the threefold goddess, the one who spends nine months of the year pregnant, giving birth to a son who evolves into the Horned God and then in turn impregnates her with himself later in the year. It would be too much for my grandmother—too much body in it, the goddess stomach swelling for more months than it spends flat.

She would stick with folks like Madame Blavatsky, with Andrew Jackson Davis, with Simon, if he's there, for her social life. I expect she'd have family members she wanted to see, but I know so little of that. And us—did she welcome my mother at my mother's passing over? Her other children and the grandchildren who've died? Will she still tell me stories she didn't tell anyone else? I believe she loved us but it's hard to know how deeply we penetrated her desires.

Given how my grandmother was always ready to be gone. Various Radfords scattered and she visited, like a niece who had moved to Kenya during a time of colonialist flocking. Another niece was murdered by gun in Beirut, by, my grandmother told me, her married lover's wife. I don't know whether my grandmother made it to Beirut before she died. In any case, *my* aunt in her crying sensed that, whether her mother cooked for boarders or while laying herself to rest in a brothel, she was always more absent than she was present.

May I think loved the version of herself she could be without ties, those ordinarinesses that yoke us: children, a person you live with whose paycheck gives you the money to survive, a living space, some set of rooms. I imagine her traveling without her wedding ring (how could you check into a brothel with a wedding ring?), reinventing herself with each change, as she did even at home: the impoverished widow, the upper-crust Englishwoman, the metaphysician. She made her own world. We were jealous of her soul, of her dealings with her soul.

MY GRANDMOTHER AND MADAME BLAVATSKY IN HEAVEN, KNOWN AS THE SUMMER LAND

That it was a world like this one, only better. Like a postwar housing project. These were two formidable women, women who had in a sense played tricks to get the life they wanted. Madame Helena Petrovna Blavatsky founded the Theosophical Society in 1875. Theosophists believe the universe overflows with occult wisdom each of us can attain for ourselves. They believe in a oneness of things and in spirits you can contact and highly evolved beings living on other planets of our solar system and elsewhere. And they believe in the immaterial-material earthly unperishing place, the Summer Land.

The Summer Land occupies a vast belt near the "grand orbit" of the Milky Way, according to Andrew Jackson Davis, in his *Stellar Key*. He was not a Theosophist, though his beliefs and Theosophy overlapped and he and Blavatsky were acquainted. *A Stellar Key* claims to be both a rational work of science and a book written in trance. Its Summer Land has high but not rugged mountains and "spiritual and ethereal rivers" mightier than the Mississippi and a peaceful lake named Mornia. And fields and blue skies and pretty clouds.

Summer Land has music and times of festival—Davis visited astrally during a festival period, he writes—so I guess there must also be an ordinary time, a time of regrouping, going back to doing the same old things, a sweeping out of the kitchen and hanging fresh towels and wondering what to defrost for dinner, in paradise.

I gather that if you lived in a house on Earth, you might live in one in the Summer Land. You might wait there until your next life is ready for you, or if you've done well in your many existences, learned what you need to know, you might stay. In some versions of events you might in this final visit to Summer Land guide other spirits who need help in the next manifestation of their lives.

You would not necessarily get reincarnated on Earth. Millions or billions of planets have life-forms. You've lived before, all over the universe. You could be housed in all manner of bodies and sent anywhere.

Andrew Jackson Davis in his book keeps calling it "the recently termed Summer Land" or the place "recently called Summer Land." Davis doesn't mention that he's the one terming it so. Rather, in an era of astronomical discovery, he implies the Summer Land too has been sighted at the end of a telescope and can be added to the list of that modernity's finds. He offers an argument for the Summer Land proceeding from inductive reasoning and science, generously offering, in spite of his own clairvoyance, not to rely on visions.

My grandmother and Madame Helena Blavatsky don't need to worry about convincing anyone of anything, though. They are where they are. They can sit and have their tea, at the edge of Lake Mornia and under the clouds. The tea leaves I suppose tell you nothing when you can look into the future yourself, as if you wandered the halls of a museum of all time. The afterlife is a prescient place. They see what's coming: computers and microchips, the last white rhino and hives emptied of bees; and then what? Nanobots whizzing through surgery in our hearts and a north pole colored in, no whiteness. And finally the end of humans' time on the planet.

In accordance with spiritualists in general, Davis preached an afterlife of a spiritualized body only, kind of an endless Christian Science. And in the Summer Land beings communicate by thought: They can choose to speak out loud, but only if they wish to.

I wonder if my grandmother has enough interest to watch us down below, as Summer Landers can do. Perhaps she's looking at our bungalows, at the uninvited winter guests.

"Of course, we're all squatters on the earth really, Helena—Madame," she says, looking out of the corners of her eyes; she appreciates being appreciated for her wit.

Really, May, says Madame Blavatsky. Or I imagine she thinks it at my grandmother rather than saying it. My grandmother would choose to speak aloud. She likes her own voice, the English accent she kept and groomed to a high polish. She used to talk about her fondness for *the art of conversation.* (The art of conversation, it's a lost art, she said.)

Madame Blavatsky preferred in life to be referred to as *HPB.* No reason to think she does not here, too, favor a genderless nickname.

Call me HPB, she thinks.

It would be very like May to point out to Madame Blavatsky the members of her own family down below. She knows Blavatsky's history and is aware the woman left behind no children. "And which of them will be joining us up here?" she muses. "There's Mary, dear Mark. Dear, dear Eddie. And that Chris. He is turning out to be clever."

Madame Blavatsky was a caustic, forceful woman, though she did say in each life we put on a new personality as we would slip on new clothes, so who knows what she's like in death. Maybe she humors my grandmother. Helena Petrovna had been a difficult child who threatened to have those who annoyed her—mostly her nurses—"tickled to death" by mean sea-spirits called in Russian *rusalkas.* The young HPB came across as aggressive and cruel. Blavatsky's mother died when the seer was a girl, saying, "Ah well, perhaps it is best that I am dying, so at least I shall be spared seeing what befalls Helena."

Madame Blavatsky was an extraordinarily powerful woman, though a report issued by Richard Hodgson and the Society for Psychical Research in 1885 did her damage, exposing tricks like holes in the ceiling through which Blavatsky had "spirit-written" letters rain down on seekers. The report called her "an accomplished but nevertheless common fraud and impostor."

Oddly enough, the Society for Psychical Research apologized for the bias of this report—Hodgson suppressed everything that supported Blavatsky's occult claims—but not for more than one hundred years, until 1986.

If Blavatsky committed fraud, it doesn't mean she didn't believe in her occult system or that she had no real visions. Rather, it seems almost certain that she did. It was a consumer culture, to be in the occult in the late nineteenth century. You couldn't just produce the news of births and deaths, the raps on the table, the initials sizzling with significance. Your followers demanded physical things, ectoplasm oozing in the air, the sounds of voices and bells. Letters handwritten on slates or paper by spirits. If you didn't provide proper manifestations, someone else would. Ectoplasms were goopy materializations, often seeming to come from the medium's body. The spiritualist explanation for them was that they allowed spirits to take on a quick form in order to speak or be seen. One medium emitted what she called an ectoplasm by hiding in her mouth, then releasing, a long cheesecloth with a rubber glove at the end.

It was understood by those present to be a spirit-arm.

Helena relaxes in the chair that accommodates its immateriality to her large and once-diseased body. Both she and my grandmother tried to ditch husbands, she her first, the much-older Nikifor Blavatsky. Both of them married the men anyway. Now in death both choose the solitary tea table, the home with only one room with a bed in it, and for one who sleeps single. I believe HPB has a desk in her house and continues with her life's work, defining Theosophy. I am not certain what my grandmother's life work was, other than overcoming the body, and so I'm not sure what she'll do in her little house in the Summer Land.

Your Simon came from India, you know, Blavatsky thinks at my grandmother.

"Oh I don't think so," says May.

MIND

I wonder that as a child I did not absorb more of my grandmother's theological ramblings. I was terrified of death then, at least, of violent death. I worried equally about monsters and human killers, whether it was the malignant ghosts that blew out of the cemetery across the street from our apartment, or the man who butchered eight nurses one by one in Chicago, or the stranger who murdered a young girl nearby in Elizabeth. That cemetery, the Evergreen, had had multiple murders in it, the reason Chris and I were forbidden to go there by ourselves, though we did, often, to play. I went with Chris or alone, happily, then later when I tried to sleep the place pressed in on me, the un-embodied names spelled in moss, that green breathing.

The fear came at night, a wide-awake terror that bounced my heart against my rib cage. I heard hands rattling the windows, creaks on the steps when we moved into a house. I heard breaths and saw bodies shadowed in the dark. I once terrified my brother by telling him I'd found ladder marks in the ground under our window.

A painful death spooked me, but more than that, I was terrified by a death brought about intentionally, by someone or something else. I heard murmurs about the cemetery, read news stories of other murders—the Richard Speck murder of student nurses, the stabbing death of a child near me—over and over. These kinds of random murders were new to us as a country and we did a fair amount of cultural wallowing, at the time, in the question of why people suddenly might want to harm random strangers. To me the thought of someone wanting me dead felt obscurely far worse than being dead, a kind of existential juju that made the act of dying almost an afterthought.

My grandmother had taught me a habit of deep and all-consuming imagination. I could not, unlike her for most of her life, control what poured itself into mine.

WENDY

The girl, Wendy Sue Wolin, was seven, two years younger than me. She waited at the curb in front of her apartment as her mother pulled the car around. (Onlookers described her as "skipping" to the corner.) Errands to run, the child young and it's after school, so she has to be taken along. It's common— a mother in the car with her child, out doing things the child doesn't really understand, though the mother will mutter a list to her: the grocery store, the butcher. The Hallmark store, cards to tell people what a mother is thinking.

The apartment named *Pierce Manor.* And I am sorry for this. Too neat, like the graveyard across the street from my apartment. My early life fell into me as if it came from a book, not a very good one. If I'd understood *strained coincidence* and *foreshadowing* I would have worked harder to forget the details.

Newspapers would call her an *Elizabethan girl.* Every paper referred to her as *skinny.* I can see how, historically, I would have looked—thin, Elizabethan: like a piece of theater.

It could be a treat, then, for a woman to leave the house— much more came to the women in their apartments then: from the milk man; the Fuller Brush man with his stiff brushes and his soaps; the Swan.

This was my mother's life, but she didn't drive. Nor did she sit with the other wives on the apartment stoops in the evenings, painting fingernails and hollering at children. But she would brush a hand across the coffee table, she would comb her hair and purse her lips at herself in the mirror.

So Wendy stood, stopped in her obedience, a few miles away from me in a warm March in 1966. Wendy's mother curving around. A man, white, middle-aged, in a green fedora and corduroy coat, his arm drawing out toward the girl and then—*A man punched me,* she said. He vanished like something the crowd collectively made, unmade.

The man had had a hunting knife that cost him a dollar-fifty. Police found it later, cleaned. It was not a punch. The body can take time to understand.

Some people walked Wendy to a fire station across the street. They pulled the girl's coat open, loosed the hidden testimony of her blood. She died soon after. It was midday, crowded. Still, the killer melted off, and survived, with this memory, this one day with its act more focused, truer to intent, than any other he has likely known: the simple economical blow, the palmed knife. Jowly, well dressed, the kind of man I'd have hit up for change, later in my life, when I begged, drugged-out, on the street. Eyes that looked absent, tired, to me, like a doctor's.

He attacked other girls. All in one day; failed to kill the others, though he blacked a little girl's eye. He may have stabbed to death another little girl, Mae Rubenstein, the year before, in nearby Highland Park. A friend of the dead child's identified the police sketch as little Mae's killer.

Soon my town wore his face on telephone poles and trees, black-and-white fliers, with his bland face and the legend "This Man Is a Childkiller" under it. My mother walked me to school every day, then grew tired, and left me to myself. With my soft abdomen, this need I could feel on the wind.

My father told me once that he would go out driving at night cruising the roads of Elizabeth, hoping to find the man. *I wanted to find that animal,* he told me, and I remembered him pacing our apartment, the phrase *that animal* leaking from his mouth.

WANTED

The face of the man who killed Wendy Sue Wolin is one of the strongest and most accurate memories of my life. I found an image of that Wanted poster online and looked at it, some forty years after the fact, and if I could only draw, I could have drawn the man myself. I also have a clear inner picture of Wendy Wolin, clutching her stomach after the imagined punch. She has stayed with me partly due to a resemblance to myself at that age, at least me in certain photos, down to the same white barrettes holding dark curls off her cheeks. I experienced myself staring out of the photos in the paper, a confused portal.

CERN had a display in which you could see, in real time, cosmic particles hitting earth's atmosphere. They looked like spermatozoic blips. When a physicist at CERN mentioned these particles also bombarding our bodies—photons, neutrinos, muons, ten particles per second, something I knew but never pictured—my hands went to my stomach in my Elizabeth, post-Wendy stance. I did it, though it rattled me immediately that the particles would penetrate my hands.

VERTEBRAE

I've always been dogged by superstition. Some of my superstitions are time-honored ones, and some are my own. I throw salt over my left shoulder. I don't walk under ladders. But there are the ones that well up inside and then seem to become their own entity. I often when I'm speaking count syllables on my fingers, and I have to end on a pinkie or a thumb, or bad luck: I adjust the words until I do. I don't recall ever not doing this, and I feel like I should apologize to everyone I've ever talked to, for the zigzags, for the useless verbal padding. I will do this counting sometimes when I think, though not when I write. I often do it when other people speak.

I haven't in years of marriage told many of these oddities to my husband, some not until I wrote them down, and figured the game was up. It's a little out of embarrassment, but mostly the way you don't feel the need to share things you do automatically, like going to the toilet, or brushing your hair. These are my fundamental forces.

I tell Bruce one night over dinner about the counting, and the fact that I can't get off the elliptical machine at the Y unless the calories burned is some multiple of five. He points out the obvious, that I have a thing for orders of five. I am stupidly surprised to think of matters this way. I like other numbers, particularly 9, but have no feelings about 5. I've since thought about this but have no idea what it means.

I played solitaire once or twice on my Kindle while reading the paper in the morning, and then it became a rule—I had to play solitaire in the morning, and I couldn't stop until I achieved solitaire in a certain length of time. If the cards are perverse, I run late. I didn't mean to get myself into this behavior. I don't recall when it started or when it became so absolute. That's the nature of superstitions: They creep and they grow.

I recall my mother having her superstitions, like the salt one, and I also remember her having very strong feelings about what you could or couldn't put on beds: no hats or no shoes, maybe both. I lay nothing on the bed except clothing and books. This way of thinking of the world—occult, full of secret levers that heave the good or the bad at you—probably came to her from both her mother and her father. She got less and less superstitious as she aged, unlike her daughter.

As far back as I can remember, I couldn't step on cracks. I didn't want to be responsible for breaking my mother's back. I expect this connects with ways in which I wanted to break her back sometimes.

I interpret cracks only as the lines that delineate the edges of concrete squares on the sidewalk. Incidental cracks due to old cement or cracks off the sidewalk don't matter. I followed this rule my entire life, which led to a certain amount of striding mixed with short minces on my walks, something that I'm sure has puzzled my little dog. I never stopped avoiding the cracks, though I understand the superstition's due to a randomness of language, and if *crack* didn't rhyme with *back,* nobody would worry about how cracks might interact with a mother's vertebrae at all.

Then my mother died and I realized on a walk that not only was I stepping on cracks, my feet were almost on their own seeking them out, leading to another kind of hopping and leaping, and probably still in the same way confusing my dog.

Superstition functions like religion, stripped of all the larger ideas. Shorn of the need to persuade. It's dogma with nothing to sustain it, so it can't ever collapse. You believe simply because you, simply, believe. There will always be luck, good and bad, enough to sustain you. Luck doesn't trade in virtue or evil. There's no one or nothing you have to love.

MAYISM

I've read *Science and Health* several times and been to Christian Science services, and I find the whole thing, with apologies to Mrs. Eddy, quite the mind-fuck. Combatting disease gets presented as less faith than battle: "Denial of the claims of matter is a great step towards the joys of Spirit, towards human freedom and the final triumph over the body," Eddy's book cackles.

May raised her children Christian Scientist, and I actually have no idea if or when my mother and her siblings got medical care growing up. I've asked my father this question but he doesn't know. I asked my mother many times when she was alive, and she always responded with, "Well, my father didn't hold with that."

"With what?"

"All that Christian Science business." My mother would be looking away, or grabbing a dish towel, or examining her hem about now. She hated discussing her mother's religion.

"So he got you medical care? Or he made Grandma take you?"

At this point in the conversation my mother would shrug helplessly. "He just didn't hold with it."

My mother remained for most of her life a person who treated a trip to the doctor the way I imagine serial adulterers treat trysts—as something she recognized she'd do but that she sure as hell wasn't going to talk about. She would leave the house for an "appointment" and even when health problems came up, never mention them unless she absolutely had to. Once she blurted out to my father that she had breast cancer and needed a mastectomy. All the visits and diagnoses had taken place without his knowledge. (My father insisted on another opinion, and she did not have cancer, luckily finding this out before losing pieces of her body.)

My grandmother did not get medical treatment, not until the time close to her death. She would be angry if she saw me with antibiotics as a child and urge me not to take them. On the other hand, she smoked, drank, and held séances, all of which Christian Science strictly forbids. Mary Baker Eddy called séances the work of "tricksters." She called spiritualism not only "erroneous" but the "offspring of the physical senses," about the most damning thing Eddy could say. I expect she found in Christian Science the closest faith she could find in New York and New Jersey, where she lived as an adult, to what she herself believed, and therefore picked and chose among its doctrines. But finally she did not want to triumph over her body, but with it, in an exalted form.

In the early days of Christian Science people called it *Eddyism*. I believe my grandmother practiced *Mayism*. Where the faith clicked with her was not in its penalties and pruderies—of which it has many—but in its tale of the absence of a true body. Her real belief was in immateriality. Her real belief was in the closeness of utopia.

"The world is perfect," she told me. "We simply don't see it, do we?"

We, not God and not the world, were the imperfections.

This is what she had learned from Mary Baker Eddy and wanted to pass on. We just needed to learn to see this way.

POINT NO POINT

George Vancouver, the British explorer who mapped the Pacific Northwest where I live, like my grandmother, began this earthly voyage in King's Lynn, England. Some biographers say Vancouver had bipolar disorder, and that place names he gave to the geographies of this region reflect his moods: Point No Point, Desolation Sound, Deception Pass. I can't speak to the truth of this but when we moved here in the early 1990s, Bruce and I took car trips around the coast. We drove to Point No Point, a two-hour jounce down a rough dirt road, just to stand on it. It all had the feeling of a Pilgrim's Progress, just, as Captain Vancouver predicted, without any point.

Like many manic-depressive people—like me, often—Vancouver had a restless spirit and could not stay put. He sailed to Australia with Captain Cook, to Hawaii, to Mexico, and Alaska. With him went the gene my grandfather also carried, the bipolar disorder gene. In my grandfather this tendency took the form of melancholy. In my grandfather's mother, my great-grandmother Berenda, mania led her to promiscuity (with soldiers, according to my mother's cousin Michael, who grew up in Barbados), and the breeding and neglect of fourteen children, with any or none of whom she might travel between Barbados and the US again and again. According to my Uncle Eddie my grandfather was raised partly by family friends, including two ship captains named Archer and Pilcher (why them? Could one of them secretly have been his father? Ship captains hardly seem likely candidates for foster care.).

Berenda left her legacy to three of her son Louis's eight grandchildren—Mark, Melinda, and myself. When I visited Barbados with Helen all my relatives talked about Berenda's insanity, revolving their fingers at their own heads. A brain like a whirlpool, or something in an eggbeater, caught.

AFTERMATH

I have had inaccessible spots in my brain since shock, spots that feel like walled-off cognitive cities that don't plan to open their doors again. In the hospital I saw this happen to other women getting shock—a loopy lethargy, an inability to place basic things like family members' names. Lawrence Olivier said of his wife Vivien Leigh that after shock treatment, she was simply a different being.

My gaps are particularly bad in the areas of spatial relationships and math, two things I didn't have great gifts for beforehand. These shutoffs occurred after my second or third course of inpatient shock treatment and have remained, not like drug blackouts, but long-term gaps particular to shock. Only after living in my present house for many years, for instance, did I master the names of my two cross streets. Before, they would swirl around in my head with similar street names if I tried to recall them (and rather than delete and replace this I'm going to tell you that when I told my husband a few days ago that I'd finally learned our cross streets, he said no, I still got one of them wrong).

I have to tell people to use their GPS devices if they ask me directions, even for places within a mile of my home. Questions about basic addition beyond the number 8 ping against the place in the brain I sense knows them easily, while the rest of my brain struggles, counting the numbers one at a time on my fingers: eight plus five is eight, nine, ten, eleven, twelve, thirteen. Is that five numbers? Yes it is.

I have GPS on my phone too, and calculators, and I'm not really complaining. That you would *forget* with shock I can understand. That in the brain's many fiefdoms of cognitive processes several would shut themselves off feels weirder, as if those electrons ripped down the connections like a windstorm downing power lines. Or more like that medieval shutting of the city gates as people hear the plague coming, but in this case, after health returns they can't open them again. Still, these places are present, present and inaccessible, not precisely the same as gone.

DIY

At the shore we lived a mile and a half from the nearest grocery and none of the Boxill sisters—the only ones down there during the week besides kids and sometimes grandparents—knew how to drive. My grandmother did not drive, and my grandfather could but did as little as possible. My mother and her sisters finally learned in their forties, but even when they could drive, none of them liked to. And my grandparents in their different ways were remarkably able, which explains how we lived in the summer, with a lot of foraging and a lot of do-it-yourself, before DIY became a thing people wanted to do.

My grandmother taught my cousins and me to recognize sassafras saplings, and I still want to pull at the saplings when I see that leaf pattern: three different leaves—single-lobed, double-lobed, and tri-lobed—fat and nodding off a smooth stalk. I want to chew them again, that root that tastes of soda with a back note of dirt. We dug the roots and threw them in a pail (it was, come to think of it, hard to get out of that house without a pail or coffee can, and a forage order pressed on you) and my grandfather brewed quantities of root beer, far more potent than the kind you can buy. My grandmother and my mother and aunts also taught us to find rose hips, wild strawberries, and wild beach plums, which we ate out of hand and in jams and jellies. Most of our beach plums came from a protected stretch of Long Beach Island that was a sanctuary where it was illegal to go, let alone to pick. My family had a keen regard for the law that couldn't quite hold up to the promise of fruit.

We caught or bought mossbunkers, a slow and stupid bottom feeding fish, to use as bait for crab traps. We caught and ate crabs and fished, mostly for blowfish but also for snapper and fluke. Several of us tried gardens but nothing would grow in that soil. One summer my Aunt Kathleen teased out of the ground three or four stalks of corn, the ears wizened, just a few inches long, and unearthly sweet.

I had cleaned so many blue-claw crabs by thirteen, the age at which I became feral, that I've never touched a crab since if I have to be part of the dismantling. When any member of the family caught crabs, which someone did every week or so, we'd cover the oilclothed dining table with newspaper and the kids would clean for hours, until the salt water stung, piercing the fingertips and cuticles. Crab cleaning was our job, like boiling the water after dinner and washing the dishes, tending to the littler cousins, hulling strawberries, bottom painting the boats, and a hundred other things were our jobs. We painted both bungalows and helped build the toilet in the smaller one.

My cousin Mark during the crab cleaning told us stories of the "dead men": The gills of the crab he told us were a poison that would kill us if they so much as touched our lips, or if a hand that touched them touched our lips. We scraped them off, grayish sacs, with a spoon.

"You've got dead men on your hands."

I stared at my fingers, too lubricated in crab gut to be sure.

I believed these gills were poisonous well into my adulthood, though I must have put them in my mouth one way or another many times. They taste of spoiled fish, with a wretched slimy texture, but are safe, though I think there's a human drive to want your food to dare you like that. We half-believed our blowfish had toxic livers like their puffer fish cousin in Japan, the fugu. Mark and Chris would tell us this and we girls made no effort to find out the truth. Nor did we think about it much when cleaning the fish, slitting their bellies and spilling the guts like you'd shake out a purse, hacking off filets. They're small and it took three or four fish to feed one person. We cleaned quickly and weren't careful.

I do remember many nights at the shore in my top bunk on the right side of the bunk-bed room, wondering if I was going to die before morning. Three cousins would be in the room with me, their deep and even breathing saying *This is being alive, what you have to lose.* I did not imagine a Summer Land or anything like it. I felt that enormous darkness rear back and ready itself to swallow one thing more.

I don't recall blaming the familiar crabs or fish for my coming death, though at times I expect I did. I focused on Mark's stories of giant mosquitoes that had mutated due to radiation from the nearby nuclear power plant and drained humans of all their blood in one suck, and how the shuffling sound of someone walking on the road in front of our house seemed to loop in closer and closer.

To fear death; to do nothing to avoid it. This seems very characteristic of all of us.

The word we used most often at the shore was *jury-rigged.* The term dates back to the 1600s, the time when my ancestors came to Barbados (and they probably also used the heck out of it). *Jury* is correct, and the common substitution of *jerry-rigged* is an error, a confusion with *jerry-built. Jury* in this sense means makeshift, temporary, not good, but enough for the moment.

We jury-rigged pipes to keep the well my grandfather dug pumping up water, and we jury-rigged fixes to our crab nets from someone's knitting, and we jury-rigged tables from driftwood, and a diaper for the newest baby out of towels. Our place was contingent, leaking, rusting: pipes burst under the house, pilot lights flicked out, toddlers puked and peed and skinned their knees on the rocks in the road, power snapped off so we sighed and lit kerosene lamps. People from Barbados are famous for this: making do. Using what we have and getting the best we can from it and not expecting too much. No one in the family ever argued that blowfish, which we rolled in flour and fried, was actually good. It tasted like nothing really. It just *was,* the alternative to no dinner.

And I gather people who make do with what they have also make do with what kids they have: We were bodies put together for work, feet that could stamp a shovel or pull groceries for a mile and a half in a metal pull cart, hands that could stroke a paintbrush, pick and dismantle.

I did not hear of myself then many compliments that could not equally be paid to a draft horse, particularly from my mother. I was "sturdy," she liked to say, with "eagle eyes" and "strong teeth that weren't likely to give trouble." When asked if I could do something, my mother would answer that yes, I could, because I was a *big bouncer.* "I'll send Susanne over," she said to my Aunt Catherine, when my aunt called to get gardening help, which she regularly did. "She's a big bouncer." She loaned me out to our elderly neighbor, saying the same thing.

I took the compliment, and have appreciated, as an adult, what the family gave me: the sense that there's no good reason something I need or want, like root beer, shouldn't come to me through the effort of my own hands.

A THOUGHT EXPERIMENT

Helen and I played a game called The Man from U. N. C. L. E., after the television show. Like many cousin-games this one had no rules and looked in many ways identical to living our lives.

We did just what we'd be doing—swimming, rowing, stomping cattails—but as we did whatever, we carried on conversations with an imaginary Napoleon Solo and Ilya Kuryakin, the show's leads. The men were handsome spies. Ilya was Helen's; Napoleon was mine. Light-haired men always were Helen's, and mine the darker. These things were known.

We said things like *Ilya, is that a KGB agent, that man with a snick in his tooth?* and *Sit down Napoleon or the boat will tip,* and then we said *Ewwww, he's kissing me again.* We said this as we walked and rowed and as we swam with them in the sargasso-ed water without clothes. At times we woke up in the morning sweat-soaked and said *Ewwww, he's been kissing me all night,* and pretended to wipe saliva off our legs and arms and everywhere. We did not need to say we woke up still playing the game. This too was known.

Let me see: There was sex, which we vaguely understood but couldn't get the mechanics of (I had glimpsed full penises and couldn't find a space in my body big enough to fit them, no matter what people said) and in which we had no interest, and then there was a dark, juddering thing having to do with the lower body. It in no way resembled the sex of the adult world; warm and spread, not genital. It had to do with being wanted but didn't end there. It held a fizz. Genitals were for some shapeless future. This pleasure was ours. It began at the body but went on and on, like the heavens we lay on the roof of the Little Bungalow to see at night, lying on our backs staring at the dark punctuated by constellations because its infinity created a heave that felt like falling.

Stars shone white-bright at first but as we looked we could see color—rose, blue, yellow, and our favorite, aquamarine—the color shining through the starlight like matches from different sets burning together, something we pyromaniacs knew very well. But matches could not stay lit.

Helen and I from early childhood on went to the bathroom together at the shore, though it was tiny, and hardly fit us both. My Aunt Catherine in particular hated this habit. Many times she told us to stop. We ignored her. *Do you have to go yet?* we'd ask the other, and if we heard *No not yet,* we said, *I'll wait.*

That's disgusting, my aunt said. *If you need to go you go,* she said. But we paid no attention, and if we had summoned them, when we finally went to the bathroom Ilya and Napoleon went too.

DR. W.

I was in a psychiatric hospital in New Jersey for five weeks. I had shock treatment there and my memory fragmented, but I held onto this fragment, of the head doctor. I—and everyone else—rarely saw Dr. W. one-on-one. He had graying hair and an impassive face and loomed far above us with a gravi-tas that only exists in asylums (a word I still find honest, with its connotations of warehousing), a cultivated sanity that could absorb any lunacies thrown its way into its chilly and rational heart. He did lead a therapy group I attended, and at one group therapy session he announced that a patient, a girl whose name I don't recall and who was mildly pretty with large breasts, would like to sleep with him and he would like to sleep with her but had decided to let us have a say in whether he in fact did.

He was middle-aged and she was a teenager and his face had the same expressionlessness posing this question that it always had. I was fifteen. I did register that I was not pretty or busty enough to be the object of this discussion. Otherwise, it felt like a question arising out of life circumstances far beyond my understanding, and the sophisticated answer seemed to be yes. I think most of us said yes, with uncertainty, as we all felt some critical test hovered at the back of the words. I assume they then had sex. I think perhaps she had been groomed by shock treatment. I don't really know.

FUTURE TENSE

I keep wanting to speak to my grandmother again, and to my mother. I want to speak to them in my garden. It's a place where time, what Albert Einstein called the "stubbornly per-sistent illusion," persists most stubbornly. Take, for instance, the daylilies, which open first thing in the morning, and close at dusk. They are yellow, stretched throats restless with ants. They nod along with the sun's passings like spectators watch-ing a particularly slow game of tennis. A week ago they had not bloomed, and two weeks from now they'll be finished. Seed-pods will come, with their dry rattle. The voodoo lily's spathe is starting to form; the arugula's bolting already and needs to be harvested.

As we exist on a fundamental level, me and the lilies and the ants, we are bundles of quantum parts and as such, we exist outside of time. We are made of atoms, and they are made of protons, neutrons, and electrons; the protons and neutrons, of quarks. There are plenty of other subatomic bits: leptons, muons, gluons, to name a few. These at the very least do not exist in any causal way that we would understand.

A 2016 physics conference posed the question of whether the future has as much validity—as much presence—as the present. Many attendees believed that it does. In one current and popular physics theory, we live in the so-called block universe, in which past, present, and future all exist at once.

At this conference physicist Bradford Skow described the experience of the present as us simply following a spotlight that moves across the block of time, sequentially highlighting what we feel as the moment. Not everyone agreed.

Physicist and philosopher Avshalom Elitzur snapped during a block universe discussion, "I don't think next Thursday has the same footing as this Thursday." Later, during another time discussion, he said, "If I bang my head against the wall, it's because I hate the future."

It would be a strange argument to have with people on the street, whether next week has as much reality as today, and an even stranger one if they then began banging their heads against a wall.

Laboratory experiments seem able to change the past of a photon, the basic wave-particle of light. This may sound absurd, but as I'll tell you in a little while, it is—though open to more than one interpretation—not absurd at all. Julian Barbour has been credited with saying in the future we will look to the future for predictions about the present, but Barbour tells me this is a little exaggerated, though he thinks "some futures are more probable than others and to that extent might be affecting the way things unfold."

It's a twisty proposition, that of a future likely enough to inflect what happens in the present. A future whose impact is felt in the present moment. And a less likely future may have less of an impact. I can't say I understand this but it makes me want to read everything that happens in my life like it's moving in several directions, even when it appears that it isn't: the loss of a set of keys; the fifty-mile-an-hour wind blasting my town at this moment, yanking the pointy boards off my wooden fence.

Robert Lanza calls time our turtle's shell. The turtle wanders around, probably at times annoyed by this heaviness and probably at times grateful for it, but never doubting the shell's need to exist, as we don't doubt our time. Our bodies have signed a pact with it, and even as they crawl through the ever-present block, they change. Telomeres, nucleotides at the end of our chromosomes, get shorter and more frayed as we age, meaning cell reproduction fails slowly. Did we have to be made this way? We'll never know, inside the shell, snapping and fanging at a world that seems to want to take us out of the water.

Physicist Max Tegmark compares our embodied sense of space-time to the DVD of a movie (if you and I can go back in time together, please, to that era, of rental shops and DVDs and insertion and the winding. That rental shop time in its way is gone, an absence serving as metaphor for its continued presence). As we watch it we have the sense of past, present, and future evolving in the story, though the DVD itself is a unified thing, containing all, and doesn't change over the time it takes to view it.

Time then is a local feature of the particular kind of place we inhabit, like a creek or a poplar tree we happen to live by. Or a stop sign, which I suppose, in a way, it is. We sense an "arrow" or direction of time, and of causation, says Huw Price, because our minds add a subjective piece to reality, projecting onto the world an arbitrary time that comes with our bodies. Our heartbeats, our metabolisms, our body movements create our sense of time. We want to make fundamental rules out of our bodily experience of the world. To return to Skow, our bodies move that spotlight along, shoulder to the wheel, an old but apt metaphor, as time I think we'd agree burdens us.

If true, these theories of time may account for the restless way nostalgia feels, that sense of something that's irretrievably gone, and yet somehow graspable. To me this yearning for the two women in my life feels painful and also physical, an itch rising through the skin. The same for the desire to be back in Holly Park, the Holly Park that once existed, more than a theoretical spot on a theoretical block: It's a longing that feels restless, as if, if only I could want harder, I could go back. As if my body can sense the remains of things, broken down into their smallest parts, but here.

Lee Smolin would argue time is the most fundamental thing that exists and that it cannot go backward, but only forward. A minority view, but far from a minority of one. Lee would put space into the category of illusion, the illusion being the existence of an absolute space through which we move. My grandmother's Summer Land ceased to exist in time but isn't lost to a place we can view as a fixed point in the universe. That universe and its laws move and evolve and could even evolve to create an Andrew Jackson Davis Summer Land. If its evolution is infinite (and what could stop it?) it would have to.

REWINDING

As my mother died her fear of death became more and more intertwined with her memories. The past returned, alchemically changed from dross to Summer Land. Lying in her hospital bed she remembered sailing as a child in a little boat, and half-shrieked, *I never appreciated it! Never! Never!* while describing the boat, the sail, the water: staring at her children, wanting us somehow to take on her hunger for her past before it left her, or she, it.

As a child, I learned from my mother how to drink the drop at the end of the wild honeysuckle's thread-like style, carefully pinched out to leave the liquid, like a seed pearl, at the calyx's green tip. I tried sometimes to capture the drops in a cup, but that never worked. Tapped against glass, they disappeared. Honeysuckle is floral beyond imagining. Back then it made me think of the nectar of the gods. I had children's books on mythology.

Now I have honeysuckle in my garden, a showy one with three colors of flower. The plant, an invasive species that doesn't belong here now or in New Jersey back then, came with the house. But I have it by inheritance, and I taste it when the flowers cluster off. It rewinds my DVD to the Jersey shore and my grandmother who also tasted honeysuckle and who did not believe in death.

Or not for herself. For me, for the rest of us, who knows.

SAYS

Are you there?

Simon says *Yes*. Simon's name is one of those words that has a long lineage. Used in Latin, Greek, and Hebrew, it means "to hear." He hears. *Yes* is one woody echo, one knock on the table. *No* is two. Or Simon tips himself off to the right, their signal for a silent *yes*. Simon has many ways to speak. The activity's called *table rapping* or *table tipping*. You communicate through the table knocking answers back to you, or by it tilting in designated ways. My grandmother does both things. It's a rule of table tipping and table rapping that the table must be round and large. Round and large exactly describes the table where we eat at the shore, in the living area, so the reason my grandmother chose this table instead eludes me. Either she'd developed a tipping/rapping method different from the accepted one, or she sensed Simon was in there, or that he could be coaxed into there, and coaxed out again to speak.

Simon's table is small and square, maybe three feet per side. He's coated with layers of blue paint, at least when I know him he is, when he serves as a side table in the bunk bed room, spilling with issues of *Ripley's Believe It or Not!* and *Mad* magazine and the *Monkees* magazine and *Tiger Beat*. His bumpy paint is bright, a nursery blue. There's no secret to his history—someone will say "Oh, where's that book, I must have left it on *that* table." When we ask how the houses came to be named Journey's End—we have a painted sign with this name in the front, by the oak tree that lightning has split so it grows out from the divisions—my mother says that Simon told them to name it this.

Are you there?

Oh I'm here, he says. Simon says. An otherworldly prankster? Simon says *Name your house Journey's End.* Simon says *Your first love will die in war and your second shall be. . . .*

The table answered, but do you really know who it was? *Feats of tricksters,* wrote Eddy. Perhaps the table spoke once without naming itself. And you followed directions anyway, and in some metaphysical way you lost the game.

He looks up at them, the woman with the plain patrician face, the three girls, the boy.

Has he experienced physicality before? A materiality spiritualized, as Andrew Jackson Davis would put it, circling some world in one of the rings or belts Davis so loves he finds them all over. He considers them the places the spirits prefer to live. Simon's a four-limbed body like the human one, one that floats in the air above a body of water, hears itself called, and spreads its restless presence into the table.

PART II

INTERROGATIONS

HARD PROBLEMS AND
HARDER PROBLEMS

THE RED PERCEPTION

And what do you do if she falls on her face, gets a bloody cut, as has happened?

Though my grandmother talked of the mind so much, she would never have acknowledged it could be bipolar, or schizophrenic or hyperactive or anything like that, though I cannot imagine likelier states for the God I know, the one who might be keeping the future in a block like a wrapped gift. And under every tiny something puts a tinier something to find. And the dualities. Night and day, up quarks and down quarks. Seasons that strip off each other's work. You could argue the fundamental law of the universe is the law of contradiction.

Mary Baker Eddy came from Boston, sickly as a child with possibly psychosomatic complaints, well once she jettisoned her body. I had not thought until I typed this sentence that my mother was probably named for her, but I feel certain, as I think it, that she was. This move feels intrusive and unfair in just the way my pregnant grandmother would be. Maybe it was a bit of an invocation: Mary Baker Eddy, get out of my womb and give me my not-body back again.

All is infinite Mind and its infinite manifestation, Eddy wrote, and *God is All in All.*

Eddy's body proved a hostile witness at the trial of the Lord that was her life. It testified that, given how we suffer, we can't say our God treats us as a loving parent would. Or we must doubt God's power. The unreality of the body was, really, a master stroke of theology, in an era of death by cold and flu, bloodletting, and amputation.

The more scientists and philosophers have considered it, the more consciousness studies has expanded as a field, the harder it's become to answer the question of what it means to be conscious. We may reject Eddy's conclusions about Mind, but it's hard not to get caught up in her subject matter. There's the problem of a delay researchers have found between acting and choosing to act that seems to say we act before choosing. There's the hard problem, the simple but impossible question of how cells firing all over the place inside the skull form subjective experience. Related are the binding problem—how we bind information from different centers in our brain to form one thought—and the problem of why what we perceive feels to us like it has specific qualities. We have theories that suggest consciousness has no real role in the world, except as after-the-fact inner ramblings.

And there's no answer to the question of why we experience the world from the perspective of one unified thing, one self.

Is it possible for scientists who spend so much time thinking not to think about thinking? Many physicists have joined in the search for an answer to the problem of consciousness, some theorizing that consciousness may be a quantum event. More and more natural processes, like photosynthesis, have been found to involve quantum movements.

Stanford's Andrei Linde wrote in his book *Quantum Cosmology and the Nature of Consciousness* that "it would probably be best then not to repeat old mistakes, but instead to forthrightly acknowledge that the problem of consciousness and the related problem of human life and death are not only unsolved, but at a fundamental level they are virtually completely unexamined." Indeed. Unless you count the hours we all spend waking up in the middle of the night, suddenly wondering what the world will do without us.

Mind was one of my grandmother's favorite words and I often hear it in my head in her low and precisely toned voice, but it's one she mostly uttered not in the Mary Baker Eddy sense but in the common meaning of *Watch out*: mind your manners, mind that last step before the bay, the rotten one, mind your little cousin on that step. A way of saying *Consciousness, hello*.

THE PROBLEM OF THE FIVE-HUNDRED-MILLISECOND DELAY

But how can it be like that?

In the 1960s and 1970s a physiologist named Benjamin Libet became obsessed with consciousness. This bent feels appropriate in the era of Timothy Leary and turning on, tuning in, and dropping out. Libet then created a series of (what would turn out to be) radical experiments, and he found that we humans start doing things before we have consciously decided to do them. Your brain activity reflects a choice before you yourself have made one, and the difference runs about five hundred milliseconds—half a second, give or take a little. And so your brain turns on before consciousness tunes in, and many philosophical certainties drop out.

You have begun reading this page before consciously deciding to read this page, which makes me as an author wonder if you even meant to. Maybe you'd rather be on your porch smoking a hand-rolled cigarette or doing a just-easy-enough crossword puzzle, if you could actively preempt matters and use your conscious mind to decide. If that's the case, I'm sorry.

Libet began testing the way people respond to brain signals during brain surgeries, stimulating different areas of the cortex. Intrigued by the difference between what people feel and what's happening in the brain, he created a series of experiments. Libet found that the brain state in which you are about to flex your wrist, say—the readiness potential, which I'll call the *flex-wrist go*—happens before you think, *Well, right now, it would feel pretty good to flex my wrist.* The gap between acts runs from 150 milliseconds to eight hundred, with half a second average.

It was such a perverse discovery that researchers kept retesting it, and, while there are dissenters, Libet's research has never been definitively refuted. A large body of research agrees that we begin to act before we make a conscious decision to act, and at times we seem to move without the information we need to act. Given the speed and distance of a tennis match, to give one example, players respond before consciously seeing the ball leave the server's racket.

Rather than mind controlling body, it seems that somewhere in our nerves and cells we are prescient of our own minds. This leaves us in the position of being what T. H. Huxley called "hopeless spectators" of our own lives.

Dissenters note that some of Libet's experiments relied on self-reporting, and self-reporting could itself have a delay. Or that there's a preconscious self working in the brain that's still us. A 2015 experiment designed to update Libet showed that people can "veto" the readiness potentials—the flex-wrist go—

or challenge the brain's pre-existent decision to move, as long as they do so within two hundred milliseconds of the start. This is not, however, what most of us would mean by "free will." As one researcher put it, we only seem to have "free won't."

The delay between our conscious choice of an action and our starting to perform it has led to many theories. A common one is that consciousness is an illusion, a way we narrate to ourselves a series of events and actions that have already occurred, trying to feel in control of a life we live unconsciously. We are liars, rationalizing, or zombies, but zombies with a voice-over. A thought experiment (which is a way of making a hypothesis with parameters that can only be thought, not created in a lab) asks what would be different if we lived on Zombie Earth. Nothing would be different, the answer goes. Not even the thought experiment itself, or its outcome.

Libet's research speaks to the blurring we all live between conscious and unconscious acts. It is a daily event that we drive to work or take a shower without registering that we're doing so—routines quickly fall below the conscious surface. And yet it's the same act if we do it consciously. This is one of those daily realities that can be mind-bending, if you think about them.

The great physicist Roger Penrose theorized that consciousness is a quantum event that carries information backward in time, or Penrose would say that it's not information exactly, but a shaping force. In our minds we endlessly scurry from milliseconds of the present into the near past (my grandmother sinks her knife into an apple—then notices the jam is thin).

If the quantum time travel guess is true, consciousness is either the most nifty, gee-whiz, gadget-y part of our whole apparatus, or it's less the arrow of time than a leghold trap: We get to yank backward over and over again but manage just a tiny movement.

I'm upset with you about your little cousin Nerissa, says May. *She fell down on the stairs when I told you to mind.* She sits down at the table with her first granddaughter, who is yanking off the ridiculous swim cap her mother makes her wear. It's bright yellow, with white plastic flowers whose petals flap off like peeling skin, and it makes the girl's head look small as a bird's.

THE JAM THICKENS

Jam setting falls under the mantle of classical mechanics, the world as we know it, Isaac Newton's falling apples. Pectin, whether powdered or from an apple, is a carbohydrate that meshes cell walls, causing fruits to gel. It requires acid and sugar to work but it has substance, and it causes material things to behave in a predictable manner, bits of fruit suspended in an inevitable web.

Quantum mechanics underlies Newtonian mechanics—apples are quantum particles like electrons and quarks beneath it all—but does not follow Newtonian rules, of time and place, past and present. A quark could fly any way from the tree. It's possible nothing actually exists, in the way we mean this word, except mathematics or simulation or consciousness itself. The apple itself might be an illusion.

You could call a family a quantum system, coming to be and popping out through interaction, like quantum particles, never quite in a fixed state unless banging into one another.

We don't see any of this quantum universe, though we could. Our eyes could be designed to catch the bubbling of quantum existence. As it is, the world as we see it ticks along, giving us what it teaches us to expect—the apples fall from the tree and attract the eyes of a boy. Or one softens into jam, the spoon slows.

Entangled particles that share qualities like spin or polarization exist in such a way that a change in one creates instantaneous change in the other (up-spin changing to down-spin leads to the opposite, down leading to up, in the partnered particle), even if any signal passing between them at the speed of light would take hundreds of years to arrive. Particles become entangled when they interact physically; one entanglement experiment shoots photons through a crystal, splitting them and creating paired photons. No matter where one of these particles travel, its state instantly reflects the other's. This itchy connection too feels like family.

The knowing of this world is so hard that one of the greatest physicists, Richard Feynman, begged people including and especially other physicists not to think into his field too deeply: "Do not keep saying to yourself, if you can possibly avoid it, 'But how can it be like that?' because you will get 'down the drain,' into a blind alley from which nobody has yet escaped. Nobody knows how it can be like that."

And May says, *Change into your clothes and come back. I have strawberries*—which meant the child would hull them, teeny wilds, and pretend all kinds of things to counter the small-stinged tedium: She pinches the hair off a thousand tiny heads, a red pearl lies at the heart of the rarest berry. She will almost not know she's doing it except for those little bites of pain.

Her grandmother's cheeks remind her of apples, not the deep red ones but the more mottled pink. May has defined cheekbones but they're broad and not sharp, curvy like the top of an apple. This too may occur to her.

CONSTRUCTOR THEORY

Constructor theory, developed by physicists at Oxford, is an information theory. It feels like it should have to do with Lincoln Logs or Legos, or HGTV, that channel where people take houses apart then rebuild them, refreshed and whole. It is none of these things. It aims to solve problems by changing the way we look at them. The theory does not look to initial conditions and predicting outcomes (a quarter ounce of pectin in the apple, eight cups of berries, and you get a proper set). It's a super-information theory and nonprobabilistic, so it doesn't look at cause and effect and try to figure probable results that way. The theory avoids these so-called dynamical laws and instead expresses transformations: possible tasks and impossible ones.

Constructor theory was created by physicists but applies to many other things: There's a constructor theory of evolution, which I cannot quite follow. I suppose humans could be looked at as possible transformations, and our afterlives and our environmental damage, possible transformations too.

If there is no clear law forbidding something, Chiara Marletto tells me, under constructor theory you try to enact it. This idea could be extended out of science, she says, to lead to "a kind of rationally optimistic way of life."

THE HARD PROBLEM

And what did you think *you were doing?*

David Chalmers, a philosopher of science and consciousness, came up with the term *the hard problem* to describe the problem of conscious experience. We can see much of how the brain works with tests like functional MRIs (fMRIs) showing how brain regions light up, pulsing color, as we sense and feel. But we can't explain subjectivity itself, why it feels like something real inside to watch a sunset or listen to jazz. Or the reason that brain processes only sometimes self-narrate to create an inner perception, and why they choose what they choose to perceive.

I rarely miss hearing a birdcall (and even in writing this, I realize: of course I don't know how many I miss, as I miss them, but in comparison to people around me, I tend to be the one noticing the hair-pull squawk of a Steller's jay, the one-two trill of a robin). I'm not a birder—I'm not *interested*—I just find birdcalls harder to ignore than other sounds. I can magically not hear a ringing phone, though I want to hear my phone ringing. I want to say: *But that's all trivial, it's not what makes me* me. By that I'd mean I have a sense of identity, a *me* based on qualities I find inside myself—the strange bipolar person who gardens, for example, maybe to stop her twitching fingers from counting. A superstitious granddaughter of May. A former addict, a word that derives from Latin and can mean both to consecrate or to betray. My identity has little or nothing to do with birds, in my opinion, but my opinion seems removed from what my brain does in regard to birds. My mind's values are not my brain's.

And that the soundtrack of those brain signals—erratic, chaotic, easily lost, easily falsified—comes to seem like the equivalent of a human life lived in the world: the strangest thing of all. Philosopher Thomas Nagel describes the hard problem as the fact that there is *something it feels like* to be us.

There is something it felt like to be May. I can, as a fellow conscious person, understand her as a subjective being. I think subjectivity binds us all to a degree. Though I find it likelier that I understand your, reader, notion of *sad* than your notion of *red*. My husband and I have long-running disagreements on the color blue; his blues are often, to my mind, green. My father's red is maroon, which I find brownish.

I have never had to explain *sad* to anyone, or have a person explain it to me. *Oh you're sad,* I'll say. *I'm sorry. Tell me what happened.* (Not how it feels, but how it occurred). Yet it seems as if, if we're deep, individual thinking beings, real in the sense that we have feelings and perceptions that are unique, *sad* should be harder than *red*.

The consciousness question is not as simple as that our brains light up, and we think. Our neurons do the same things whether we're functioning unconsciously or consciously, and we function unconsciously most of the time. You can do very complex things without being aware that you're doing them. This fact makes the presence of a conscious you potentially meaningless.

Even in conscious acts, our bodies seem one step ahead of our brains. And how, given that all we perceive is spread out all over the brain—color here, sound and texture elsewhere, concepts like *dog* in still another place—do we have no problem recognizing and characterizing a dog? Out walking we stop to pat one, make small talk and tell the dog's person that it looks like a Chow mix, and has very soft fur. This is one example of the binding problem, the problem of how we bind together the information we get from the cortex's many sensory fiefdoms.

Scientists want a Theory of Everything, a theory that will explain the workings of all the pieces of the universe—space-time, gravity, quantum behavior—that cannot now be reconciled. Increasingly scientists say such a Theory of Everything, or TOE, must account for consciousness too.

I think all of us crave a TOE. Life is Newtonian and yet feels quantum, everything in superposition once you live it and it pops restlessly into the past. Today for no reason my brain floods—and there's a sense of its actual presence in my olfactory spaces—with the deep burned sugar smell of the island of Barbados, from its rum plants. I traveled there as a young woman.

Why these returns, what theories do we have? There is Christian Science, there is spiritualism, there's daily life, there's physics, and there's the shore. Where toes in fact had a strong presence: dipped, crab-clipped, stepped on by brothers and cousins, occasionally victims of a dropped or thrown fire-cracker. As I recall, a Band-Aid was a staple part of the front of my feet back then, just migrating a little from time to time. All of this feels in my writer's TOE mind as if it should matter.

David Chalmers believes it's possible that consciousness is a fundamental cosmic force, joining up with electromagnetism, gravity, and the strong and weak nuclear forces. As a funda-mental force, consciousness can't be taken apart, but must be understood as a given. Donald Hoffman believes the physical universe, even the big bang, has to be understood as emerging from the fundamental ground of consciousness.

My grandmother would find these wholly Christian Science points of view. And she could probably find a coherent way to explain them. Though few scientists understand con-cepts like a fundamental ground of consciousness or a "cosmic consciousness," as Nobel Laureate Eugene Wigner worded the same idea, as religious.

Plenty of neuroscientists still believe consciousness just comes from our neural wiring—neurons, synapses, and so forth. It's an emergent property that happens when many pro-cesses come together, or an epiphenomenon, an add-on expe-rience to a lot of physical things happening, many but not all in the brain. As an epiphenomenon, consciousness doesn't have to matter, but could be the illusory voice-over theorized by scientists like Susan Blackmore, who comes from the line of thought called *illusionism.* She calls consciousness some-thing we experience, but something akin to a "visual illusion," a "mirage."

What did you think *you were doing?* This, my mother's favorite question. It was not, as it might be in the mouth of my father, a real question: It was wholly rhetorical. Asking it (maybe precipitated by something like a firecrackered toe) meant we had to consider the fact that we weren't thinking at the time of infraction. The theory seemed to be that once we realized we hadn't been thinking, we'd begin to think. We heard this question multiple times a day, so apparently the logic had its faults.

I've heard groups of cognitive theorists debate consciousness—the ones who say emergent property, the ones who say quantum process, the ones who say illusion, the ones who say fundamental force. They argue and then at some point the materialists—the ones who think consciousness can be wholly explained by what's in the brain itself—turn to the others and say, *But if I bash you in the head, you'll stop thinking.*

Meaning: If something outside your brain creates consciousness, how can I stop it so easily, with a big rock or even a piece of this sharp lectern in my hand? I might rephrase by asking why electrodes sizzling their electrical currents into conducting gel and then into your brain can change it so much.

There's really no answer to this question. The comment is an epiphenomenon of this science discussion.

VIEWS

"If the future isn't open," physicist Lee Smolin tells me over the phone, "it's an unattractive world, it's inhospitable to many of us, our picture of nature is reduced to an interaction of atoms, there's no human meaning, and free will is impossible."

I'm not being anti-punctuation here. This did come through the wire as one long dystopian sentence.

I've asked Lee to explain the ramifications of his physics thinking to those of us who simply live as homo sapiens in a confusing universe, and he gives me this answer. I'd always found the timeless universe comforting, whether I could access its tightly held riches or not. But Lee diverts my thoughts. Timelessness does strip us of our decision-making power, of the possibility that choices matter. I've considered this distinction a lot since our conversation. Some days I want the future and some days I don't. Some days I'd like to think the time I spend sorting recycling can point to a better future, even if it's the immediate future of a less-teetering landfill. Other days I'd rather think I'm not able to mess up.

I first encountered Lee's ideas in a blog he wrote for *Scientific American.* In it he described space, which he does not accept as fundamental, as an "emergent rough description" we make of what's happening to us in the universe. It arises, he said, due to "the coarseness of our sensory perceptions." I imagined my fingers, rough like the holes of a grater, running across the face of the universe. It felt in some way a beautiful thought.

Lee's work straddles quantum mechanics, relativity, and cosmology, so he spends a lot of time considering minute particles, gravity, and the universe. Other scientists share his belief in fundamental time, but Lee is an originator, and probably time's greatest advocate right now. It's not an easy lift; he himself, in his book *Time Reborn,* calls the theory of illusory time a "formidable" one to contradict.

I've been asking questions of Lee on a phone line that has interference and makes him sound like a staticky radio, a strange thought to occur when talking to a physicist, as radio static is caused by the Cosmic Microwave Background. The CMB is the radiation produced by the big bang, still out there coating the universe, and snagging up radio signals.

The larger theory Lee embeds his theory of time into—or that is generated from it—is called the *causal theory of views.* Causal view removes space as a fundamental infrastructure of the universe and makes it something that emerges from causal, or cause-and-effect, events. Lee believes gravity too emerges, rather than existing as an absolute. Emergent properties are properties that result from, to put it inelegantly, little things that aren't something clumping together into bigger things that are something. An atom of water is not wet. Wetness takes lots of atoms of water. The atoms in the letter *m* don't carry the sound of *m,* though thinking about it, I wish they did. *M* takes not just lots of atoms, but lots of atoms congregating in my laptop.

As emergent things, the universe and its laws, while predictable at any given time, evolve and change. Lee's theory is a realist theory, meaning in it the cosmos has a reality outside our heads. And a naturist theory, in that nature's laws—change and evolution—apply to the universe, too. Space is not this big *whoosh* of a thing we experience, but is discrete and has pieces, albeit unimaginably tiny pieces too fine for our grater fingers. These pieces interact with one another and create events. Parent events beget baby events, and scientists use exactly that language, parent and baby. Lee calls each event's perspective— based on the limited information it has on the universe, its causal story—its *sky.* The history of the universe is composed of the universe's views of itself, also a beautiful thought.

Of course, the universe's discrete units are impossibly small. They're measured in Planck lengths, lengths so tiny that if you tried to measure the diameter of an atom in Planck lengths, doing so would take you 10,000,000 more years than the years in the age of our universe. (Planck lengths form a kind of inverse to the large number *googolplex,* a number so high that if you wrote digits so wee they fit into Planck cubes, those digits still would not fit into the universe. Googolplex was named by mathematician Edward Kasner's nine-year-old nephew Milton, making it no doubt the most adorable thing in math.)

The theory of views feels rational and—if you can get past the sense that an event having a view implies it's standing on a beach somewhere—almost too rational to nudge in next to cosmic blocks and infinite multiverses. Events beget events and keep the whole contraption going, in the same way sex keeps our species going. Parents beget babies and those babies beget more babies and whether or not we've earned it, here we are.

Though the greater the similarity between any two views, the greater the chances of those views connecting, even if they are far apart ("nonlocal"), which feels less rational. These overlapping views explain quantum entanglement as linked perspectives, like those stories of identical twins, simultaneously dialing each other on the phone.

When I talk to Lee he tells me that, like most young physicists, he used to believe time was inessential, and even wanted it to be, yearning, as he puts it in one of his books, for "timeless truths."

What changed? Part of it, Lee answers, "was becoming a parent, especially an older parent." As he loved life more, he loved time more, which is an intuitively understandable yet contradictory thing. He became increasingly attracted to the world "actually lived in by human beings."

Lee explains that a natural universe gives us the benefit of holding us in it as natural creatures. "People who are writing computer programs conceive of us as machines," he says. "We are susceptible to being turned into machines."

Lee is not the only physicist whose conversation turns to the dangers of advanced computing, moments in my interviewing when higher-level science feels like a view, a shared perspective, entangling with stories like *The Terminator*. Maybe we are lucid in our daydreams.

Like me, although far more qualified, Lee comes to science from an esoteric background. His parents followed twentieth-century mystic George Gurdjieff, a man who makes me think of a somewhat more rational Madame Blavatsky. Born in Armenia, Gurdjieff, like Blavatsky, traveled east to countries like India and Tibet in order to spread their spiritual practices throughout the West. Gurdjieff believed people all live removed from reality and in a "waking sleep." He loved dance and used it as a path to enlightenment.

"It had a lot of fraudulent stuff, manipulation," Lee tells me of Gurdjieff's movement. "It was not a good thing to see up close." He has not, though, completely dismissed the experience. Lee is still in touch with some of Gurdjieff's original students and followers of Tibetan Buddhism, and he tells me, "some of what they teach is very true. They tell me that if you follow something for twenty-five years, you can maybe learn something." Not, I gather, something very large. It's the kind of patience it takes to imagine Planck lengths.

After we speak Lee forwards me a paper he has just written about consciousness. As the theory of causal views has it, and logic dictates, novel causal events must be extraordinarily rare. The vast majority of events in the universe are routine. Lee theorizes that the physical ground of the experience of consciousness is novel events, happening somehow within the brain. He cites another author to suggest the phosphorus in our neurons' phospholipid membranes may hold quantum movements.

What comes to the brain is the baby of a parent and has a sky. A universe self-regards and somewhere in my brain events held in phosphorus combine to create the singed cane odor of Barbados. Waves collapse. Consciousness, it strikes me, sounds an awful lot like the Summer Land. I realize that here I misuse this theoretical language entirely. Though Lee and I are talking about how we want our future to look and I am imagining I hear the big bang scratching its way into our phone call.

THE PROBLEM OF THE OBSERVER

John Archibald Wheeler (collaborator with Einstein and Niels Bohr, Manhattan Project physicist, man behind the terms *wormhole* and *black hole*) said his research life fell out into three parts: particles, fields, and finally, information. The information third, as Wheeler used the term, reflected what he called an older man's concern with understanding why we exist. It may seem strange that information could address this question, get to what God had in mind with us, as Einstein might put it. But that's physics now: Existence and observation are linked in ways that don't make obvious sense.

Quantum research opened up the importance, maybe the necessity, of quantum-level observation or measurement. John Wheeler argued for what he termed a participatory universe— one in which perception changes not just the present but the past. The universe, he said, is an "endless feedback loop." It's funny in this age of Instagram, Twitter, and Facebook, reality shows where people forage naked in the wilderness, or get naked so some guy will hand them a rose. I think all of us have become confused by this question of observership. Are we really alive if no one sees us? Is an unobserved sun still a sun? Is a Facebook post real with no likes?

THE PROBLEM OF THE TWO PATHS

The fact that measurement affects the behavior of quanta is inarguable, though you can debate the reasons why that may be, or, as many scientists do, shrug it off, claiming you can't try to explain "quantum weirdness." Or claim that there is a physical explanation. For those scientists who believe consciousness is a fundamental universal force, the role of the observer in quantum experiments generally forms part of the argument. The double-slit experiment makes it clear that whether quanta come out of the state of superposition where they exist as potentialities, whether they decohere, depends on whether or not they're measured.

In the basic double-slit experiment you shoot a quantum bit, often a photon, through two slits at a panel behind them. Photons hit the slits as waves, dividing into two waves as they pass through the two openings. As waves, the photons leave a very specific pattern on the panel—brushy, vertical clumps called *fringes*. But a detector placed at each slit will change that interference pattern to a pattern of bars on the panel, a pattern caused by particles and not waves. The act of detection seems to change the fundamental nature of things at the quantum level and cause quanta to exist in a definite state. In the words of physicist Pascual Jordan, "We ourselves produce the results." The double-slit experiment is part of the logic of John Wheeler's participatory universe.

The double slit has remained what Richard Feynman called the experiment that has in it "the heart of quantum physics" but also its "only mystery." It has different interpretations: that it privileges, even makes necessary, the observer, as even our instruments serve our senses; that quanta change in their interactions with what detects them but not in a way that means anything larger than that; that we have inadequate or interfering detectors.

Andrei Linde, who studied with Wheeler, looks at the slit results as human-centered, saying, "A recording device cannot play the role of an observer, because who will read what is written on this recording device? In order for us to see that something happens, and say to one another that something happens, you need to have a universe, you need to have a recording device, and you need to have us. It's not enough for the information to be stored somewhere, completely inaccessible to anybody. It's necessary for somebody to look at it."

Consciousness and its observations may exist in the fundamental way space-time exists, writes Linde. "What if my red, my blue, my pain, are really existing objects, not merely reflections of the really existing material world?" If only, most of us might feel, he hadn't put the pain in there.

Physicist Paul Davies describes a universe in which life and mind are seeded throughout the universe, a universe that *engineers,* in his term, its own self-awareness, and in this movement toward greater consciousness fine-tunes itself.

A basic principle of science, the Copernican principle or principle of mediocrity, holds that we humans on planet Earth cannot think of our existence as extraordinary in any way. Fine-tuning, the double slit, and other results are so problematic that for many, like Rolf Landua at CERN, the concept of the multiverse offers relief. In that thinking, so many other universes exist that we can not only find ourselves more or less coincidentally in this one without an insult to reason but also somewhere the photons are delivering every possible result with the double slit.

Still, plenty of physicists believe in some version of observation, even consciousness, as part of reality's fabric. The feedback loop needs something to provide the feedback. Quantum change requires "input from the psychological realm into the physical realm," as physicist Henry Stapp puts it, in order for the cosmos to function. This statement, though I agree with it, sounds deeply odd to me, and I imagine Sigmund Freud as Atlas, the world held on his back.

CONSCIOUS AGENTS

Donald Hoffman, who I talked with about portals and interfaces, believes consciousness is the only universal force that's
truly fundamental. Even space-time in his theories is a con-
struct, or more accurately, an interface. Otherwise, he explains
to me, we are stuck with dualistic answers: there's the world
out there, the world in here.

"We prefer," he tells me, "monistic theories." I understand
the nature of science and its drive to reduce matters to the simplest possible level, and I lean this way myself in some ways,
though in others I feel more like a Madame Blavatsky or an
Andrew Jackson Davis, wanting to create a theory of the universe that takes tens of thousands of pages and equal numbers
of peoples and cosmic locations and rays.

Don tells me he thinks this way because "if we assume
senses evolved by natural selection all the predicates of space
and time aren't adequate. There's no way to see and understand
what reality is."

Evolution, as I've said, favors reducing complexity. Don has
put together a theory of the universe that has it centered on
conscious agents, those being any presence that can take action
or make decisions. There's no need for a conscious agent to
have a sense of self or memory or intelligence. This idea could
put humans and computers into the same matrix (and while it
may feel that humans are a single conscious agent, Hoffman
reminds me that people who get the connecting band—the
corpus callosum—between brain hemispheres surgically severed become independent operators, and you end up with two
conscious agents in there.)

It is weeping rain one day as I talk to Don on the phone,
weeping being the word that pushes itself into my head, and
my imposition on the portal that is rain. Or you could say
the metaphor is a portal to my sense that the rain falls slow

and slanted into tears against my window. My gray, striped cat, Friend—named for my mother's shy cousin Friend Boxill—walks back and forth on me and on my computer screen, wanting all my attention, which is normal.

"We have to accept that the universe is something new, not the one we think we know," I hear from Don, and try to picture all these presences as flattened, simplified in the manner of written language (which I am simultaneously producing, trying to hold a world in tiny curves and sticks).

The theory of conscious agents is supported by mathematical equations, which don't even serve as portals for me.

At the end of our conversation Don tells me he's working on a "mathematically precise theory of spirituality." A spiritual over-presence or God-figure would consist of infinite conscious agents. I tell him my grandmother would adore him and also that I think it's brave to head into science with such a project, though many scientists are brushing up against those questions, one way or another.

"Science is a method of inquiry," says Don. "When it comes to religion, people have been killing each other forever over this. I say, why not use our methods."

THE PROBLEM OF THE PAST

John Wheeler's delayed-choice experiment, which implied that observation can not only change the present but the past, began life as an idea: a galaxy-scale, double-slit experiment with photons passing quasars. Quasars are mysterious. We know they're distant, massive, and bright, probably drawing their energy from black holes. They can be a trillion times more luminous than our sun. The route the photon takes around the quasar is only fixed when its travel is measured, though the measurement happens when the photon arrives and not before.

After Wheeler, delayed choice became a laboratory experiment, an amplification of the double slit. There are many forms of this experiment now, but the simplest one to explain is a version where you have a beam splitter set after the first two slits, and you shoot photons at it. The beam splitter sends the photons to a mirror and produces particle behavior. The photon will then go in one path or another as a particle, hitting one of two different detectors. But if you add a second beam splitter, the photons behave as waves, and the interference pattern shows that they have retroactively behaved as waves.

Delayed choice can be hypothesized as stemming from forces other than what's called retrocausality or as our detectors persuading photons to go back in time and change their form. As with the double slit, it could be that photons are always both wave and particle and our detection systems can't see that. But no one has yet ruled out retrocausality, the present changing the past.

The interferometer used for delayed-choice and many double-slit experiments was invented in the nineteenth century by two men named Michelson and Morley, and the one we use now is pretty much the same device, a system of mirrors and detectors that merges more than one light source and looks for patterns. Michelson and Morley fired up their interferometer in 1889, expecting to find a substance first predicted by Aristotle called the *luminiferous ether*. People believed this ether allowed the universe's light to come to be, a problem then, as light seemed to have no cosmic parent. They never found the ether, a theory that had held sway for more than a millennia and a half. This fact I suppose should give all of science some pause.

We live in the forward-moving arrow of time, or we feel that way, so it's hard to say what this delayed-choice uncertainty means for a human individual. All I can tell you is that many physicists who study time come to see the past the way a restless interior decorator might see a room. Here are brocade chairs, under the gilt mirror, and opposite the painting of a ship—real things—but all of it could be moved anywhere, could have been nudged anywhere infinite times.

"The answer to the question, 'Could the world be such that we do have a limited amount of control over the past,'" Huw Price says, "is yes." Andrei Linde says, "To ask what is before this moment is a self-contradiction." Any past compatible with the present moment is a possible past.

PHI

Giulio Tononi, a neuroscientist who holds two endowed chairs at the University of Wisconsin–Madison, has developed a theory called the integrated information theory, which posits that we can measure consciousness by a unit called *phi*. Giulio looks very Nordic and has straight, blond hair, the kind of blond that's a little shiny, topping chiseled features. He is Italian though, and speaks with a passion and volubility my own Italian family has when talking about pretty much any subject at all. He's very willing to stake claims.

"We have learned so well from science that this universe is immensely grand and we are a peripheral speck, a small species on a provincial planet," he tells me suddenly over Skype. "But we exist so much more than that damn universe out there."

I'm at this time dealing with a medication change—my cholesterol has been sky-high-ing, a common side effect of antipsychotics. Now I'm having mood swings and anxiety that makes my heart, even in the *now* of the interview, feel like a bunch of hamsters are trying to eat their way out of my chest. I'm not sure I feel I exist at all. I try to imagine the most immensely grand-ish thing I can. I think of lying on my back on the roof at the shore, watching Orion, my favorite constellation, that geometric warrior fluffed with clouds and pinned to the sky.

This thought doesn't help. I feel Orion's more likely to grasp his star-sword and cut a swath through those clouds than I am to exist more than him.

Yet, I can't get away from the fact that Tononi's theories have answers to problems. Phi is a very complex theory, he tells me, which he usually only presents in multiday workshops. But I can grasp the basics. Integrated information theory and phi are a way to deal with the hard problem, this "marvelous job," as Tononi puts it, our brains can accomplish, of producing consciousness. Not only can we not explain this, as I've said, but answers only get further away as our methods of measuring brain activity get drastically better.

Most people and many neuroscientists believe consciousness is just lots of neurons and dendrites and axons working together. This theory does have problems though, the kind science does not like—the cerebellum has far more neurons than the cerebral cortex, for instance, and the gut has tens of millions too, and holds most of the body/brain's serotonin. Yet the cerebellum and the gut cannot think, while the cortex does. And as I've said, we cannot find any action in the brain that explains consciousness, the way studying the heart explains how it pumps. Though not, I recall to myself, how it hamsters.

The brain is a physical substrate of consciousness to Tononi, but it is not consciousness itself, which spreads beyond the brain and beyond us. The cortex represents trillions of phi, but in his theory, many things besides us in the universe can have phi. Even a single neuron, as Tononi puts it, would not be "nonzero" in phi. (Phi proponents and scientists in general have a weakness for the double negative.)

Tononi believes even a quantum particle like an electron could have its own little bit of phi. It helps in understanding this that Tononi does not equate consciousness with intelligence. Phi indicates a system has certain characteristics, one of which is integration, another of which is information; these two are fundamental for phi. Integration means experience must be singular and cannot be broken apart. I cannot fragment my experience of the sky into pieces, not unless I close my eyes to turn Orion into a soft blur, which I used to do (to be fair, this doesn't count, as I've simply changed the parameters of the one experience). I could not count planets and perceive nothing else. So surprising things have phi, but not everything.

"You live under a mountain," Tononi says, referring to Bellingham, Washington's, Mount Baker. "The mountain might make you feel small. But it is small, not you. It is non-phi."

A camera sensor with thousands of photodiodes would not have phi. The photodiodes would have a fleck of it, as each has a unitary experience of distinguishing between darkness and light.

Phi gives everything in the universe at least a shot at consciousness. The belief that there may be conscious existence throughout the universe is called *panpsychism*—which translates to *mind is everywhere*; *pan* for all, *psych* for mind. Tononi writes that his theories "validate some of the intuitions" of panpsychism but are not all in on that. A subset of this panpsychism is *panprotopsychism,* which means, in David Chalmer's words, that "fundamental entities are protoconscious, that is, that they have certain special properties that are precursors to consciousness." Phi split up into particles of phi.

A diode, a few neurons, might have one phi or a few hundred. Not enough, Tononi tells me, to matter a whole lot. But I wonder.

Tononi's theory rules out consciousness in computers. They do not meet his criteria. In fact, Tononi hates the whole idea of conscious computers.

"I am *worried* about this [computers]," he says. "If we get computers very functional, if they look nice, we'll want to be with them, we'll want to have dinner with them. Who wants to be with the spouse who tells the same old stories? Computers are getting better and better."

And then, he says if artificial intelligence multiplies and takes over, the universe will be gone. "The world would become essentially nothing at all. We see the beauty of a sunset. Without that seeing, the world wouldn't exist. This is as deep as it gets."

This is when Tononi, who's now become Giulio to me, tells me we exist "so much more than that damn universe out there."

Giulio is also deeply opposed to physicalism.

"Physicalists, they have sold out their soul," he tells me. "And they've sold it out to nothing."

LOOK

I would have grasped the observer principle as a child. Children understand that nothing they do is real unless watched, and so they say *look, look, look, look, look,* over and over (at me on the swings! at my hangnail! at this inchworm here in my palm). They will repeat, with a quantum sense of completion, any action that hasn't been observed, until it is.

Look, look. How I swam past the rope. How I smeared your lipstick on my own lips.

THE WAVE FUNCTION COLLAPSE

I remember feeling as a child that, though I needed to be watched to be real, adults were the opposite: most real when you saw them and they didn't know. As they looked into mirrors, maybe. Like my mother standing in front of a mirror filling in her lips from a tube of coral before the Fuller Brush man visited our apartment. That mirror-face was not a face I saw elsewhere: tremulous, leaky. She'd tilt both sides of her face at the mirror, one after another, with scrutiny, as if her face were a thing that might have changed on her since she last looked.

There were other men who came, like the man from Swans Dry Cleaners bearing my father's shirts, pinned to stiff cardboard. I got the job of removing the pins and the bonus of keeping the shirt cardboards to scribble on. My mother called the men by their trades—*the Swan man, the Fuller Brush man*—though she must have known their names. She would tell me in the morning they were coming, signaling a small but definable change in our day: hers, mine, my brother's. She would not leave our apartment until the man showed up. I might get handed a rag for dusting.

My father kept the bathroom door open during his morning rituals of shaving with Noxzema from the cobalt jar, then clipping his mustache with a scissor, calming his black hair with Vitalis. He wore his hair in two gelled waves from a middle part. He has dark skin and a broad face with a prominent nose, a face that looks more Turkish than Italian. His mirror-face looked vexed, like he and his creams and blades engaged in pitched battle against what his hair and skin would like to do.

When my grandmother looked at herself in the mirror, which she did not do very often, her face relaxed into a small smile. She was not particularly pretty, and I don't think she thought she was. She appeared to be checking in with her own existence. That, it seemed, was fine.

THE PROBLEM OF ZOMBIES

Oddly enough, philosophers and scientists of consciousness who don't believe thought exists in any meaningful way still solve problems with thought experiments. In a thought experiment, you set up a set of imaginary circumstances and manipulate them to prove something. These proofs often deal with possibility. Could a pig fly? Yes: Given a different conformation of the pig, a different aerodynamics, a pig could fly. Could a circle be a square? No. Pigs are contingent, geometry is not. Wheeler's quasar-driven delayed choice was a thought experiment.

A popular thought experiment posits an Earth populated by zombies. Unlike pop culture zombies, philosophical zombies, as they're called, aren't decaying lurchers but look like normal humans. They have intelligence and volition and do what we do, without what we call consciousness. They slurp soup, work as accountants, watch Super Bowls. They could even spend hours discussing consciousness. What they would lack is feeling, inner narration. *Qualia,* to use the technical term for the subjective part of sense perception. The thing that makes your red not my red.

What would look different? asks the thought experiment (and just for fun, someone will often throw in, *How do we know we're not all zombies?* or *I'm not the only non-zombie?* But I'll stop with just a planet of zombies). It's hard to say what would look different. Really there's nothing obvious, which is taken as proof that we can't explain consciousness in physical, strictly material, terms.

As it seems that we act before we make the decision to act, we can theorize even without zombies, consciousness may be no more than a chatty rationalization, an illusion of control. It may be the kind of lying a child does when he hits the lying age, around three or four, in love with his ability to invent, not yet realizing how obvious the inventions are. Caught with his hand in the jar of candy he might say, as my son once did, "I heard a mouse in there and had to get it out," a narration seemingly plausible, but not at all convincing.

Philosopher Philip Goff writes "Consciousness seems to be the one bit of left-over magic that refuses to be physicalized. And it's all the fault of the zombies. There is a broad consensus amongst philosophers that the *mere possibility* of zombies is inconsistent with physicalism being true." Goff means that if nothing would change if we didn't have consciousness as we know it—the inner narration—then there must be something more to consciousness than neurons and synapses, what tech people call *wetware*. Many neuroscientists have the truly terrible habit of calling the something extra *special sauce*.

THE TERRIBLE UNLIKELIHOOD OF OUR BEING HERE

Robert Lanza calls his version of the anthropic principle *biocentrism*. The universe, he says, creates sentient life because that is what it means to do. He too points to its extreme fine-tuning for life, writing, "If the big bang had been one-part-in-a billion more powerful, it would have rushed out too fast for the galaxies to form and for life to begin. If the strong nuclear force were decreased by two percent, atomic nuclei wouldn't hold together. Hydrogen would be the only atom in the universe. If the gravitational force were decreased, stars (including the sun) would not ignite. These are just three of more than 200 physical parameters within the solar system and universe so exact that they cannot be random."

Lanza does not believe that death or time, as we understand them, are real. He claims that the very idea of "death or becoming nothing is empty of meaning. Becoming nothing may seem like a tangible concept, but it is actually as meaningless as the word 'it' in the phrase 'it's a nice day.' It appears linguistically, but not in the actual physical universe."

Lanza's conclusions put him at the far end of scientists who look at these facts, but the implications he draws have been drawn by others. The fine-tuning in the universe caused Sir Fred Hoyle, one of the twentieth century's great astronomers, to say that it made the universe appear to be a "put up job." Elaborating, he said, "A common sense interpretation of the facts suggests that a superintellect has monkeyed with physics, as well as with chemistry and biology, and that there are no blind forces worth speaking about in nature. The numbers one calculates from the facts seem to me so overwhelming as to put this conclusion almost beyond question." Hoyle was and remained an atheist.

Just one example of such a fine-tuned number is found in the cosmological constant, a cosmic force or a *vacuum energy,* that counteracts the pull of gravity. Without the cosmological constant, none of the elements created by the big bang could move apart to form the universe we know, with entities like stars and planets. Too large a cosmological constant, though, and nothing could stay together. It is a very precise number. A change to the constant of the "tiniest, tiniest bit," says physicist Leonard Susskind, and we would not be here. The energy density it took to get a workable universe that could hold together had to be fine-tuned to one part in 10 to the 120th power. It would sprain my fingers to type that number.

All the carbon, the basic molecule of life, that exists had to be created inside supernovas, dying exploding stars. Stars had to explode, and explode enough, for our basic elements to be here. For them to form and grow to supernova, which is a star's old-age death blast, took more than ten billion years. It took more than ten billion years of stellar work to create the basic building blocks of life, the proverbial one-celled organism in the ooze. This could make life seem more or less likely, depending on your level of patience.

It was physicist Michio Kaku who described the likelihood of life in the universe as like a jet airplane ripped apart by a storm, then put together again, perfectly, by the same winds.

Kaku throws out the idea that an unimaginably advanced civilization runs our universe as a kind of science project. Then he sighs and says we'd still have to account for the unimaginably advanced civilization. Susskind believes we are one bubble in a sea of many bubble universes (a form of the multiverse), which makes me think of bubble wrap exploding in my son's once-tiny fingers.

Scientists use the multiverse, or bubble universes, or another variant of this theme, to explain fine-tuning—if there are infinite universes then every type is possible, and we just happen to be in this one. Paul Davies finds the multiverse theory absurd, through a series of thoughts that lead to an eerie place, though each one is reasonable: If there are infinite universes, some must be computer-generated because infinity means infinity. (There doesn't seem to be any theory that would let us have some extra universes but not a roaring lot of them.) Then because simulations are easier to create than real universes, simulations would proliferate and far outnumber the real ones. Therefore, we are likeliest to be living in a computer simulation, which means working with a simulated physics. The multiverse, he argues, ends up trying by its own logic to crack real physics with a fake one.

And there's also physicist Victor J. Stenger's dismissal of fine-tuning and observers, the universe bending its future toward an inhabited Earth, citing dinosaurs and asteroids, plagues, volcanoes, fires, and floods. "This planet," he says, "is not so great when you think about it."

PHI II

A tiptoeing silence.

You're lying on a cot on the porch. Finally the family women have driven you to bed, after you hid with your cousins on the beach, pretended you couldn't hear your yelled name, the wind batting it to your ear. Now your first impression is silence: the kind of silence that comes when you've stopped listening to yourself, not just your voice but the sounds you make with your body, no longer brushing through the cattails, stomping in the water. It's this self-silence that I think can trigger such a vulnerability; what am I, who am I, stilled?

The second thought is of sounds reassembling themselves as the sounds of *you* stop: cattails susurrate on their own, waves bang against the bulkhead, a rhythm precise—and tenacious, if you listen—as the heart's. Seagull cries erupt, moody and sometimes stricken. The world without you sounds subdued, tired maybe, but able to go on like this for a long time.

Didn't we all sense this phi once? There, where nothing is nonzero. The bay flees in circles from your ankle, the gulls complain intricately while cruising above the water. Their cries give you up, squatting on a beach chair, as your aunt crosses the street to find you. Andrew Jackson Davis called the mind "brilliant with phosphorescent illuminations," like the night water. Beach grass whips you back from the lagoon, cattails whisper as you pass through them, perhaps out of concern, or even love, a hushed shred of that.

FALLIBILISM

Most of the scientists I talk to tell me they have no idea if their theories are true. They want to test them, and if they don't test out, if the equations and proofs aren't there, move on to something else. And most would also agree that trying to put these things into language—wave function collapse, superposition, delayed choice, most things that involve physics—involves a loss. As does explanation that takes less than pages and pages of explanation and qualification, though most of the folks I talk to would not agree on exactly how that should be done. And there will still be loss.

I think of waves, which I have always lived near, and their almost-arrogant poise at the top of their swelling, then emphatic crash.

As Marletto explained fallibilism, they want to make mistakes as fast as possible and machete the brush away toward the truth. I never ask if these people wonder *What if there's no truth to be had?*

"I don't like belief," Don Hoffman told me. "I don't even believe my own theories. Respect, yes. But I don't believe."

ANOTHER THOUGHT EXPERIMENT

As a child I kept wild mice in cages in my room, once I had my own room, most of them caught but not killed by the stray cats I fed. *Look, a mouse bit me,* I told my mother one day, showing her the blood. It had, when I reached into its cage to grasp and release it.

"It'll be fine," she said, then thought about it. "Don't tell your father."

"But it broke the skin." We kids, with our muskrats and weasels and so on at the shore, knew our rabies.

"It'll be fine." She clamped down her lips. Was she having a Christian Science moment? She did not drive at this time. We never used taxicabs. Her bar for what constituted a doctor visit emergency was set high.

AFTERWARD

I expect that my fear of death kicked in this night of the mouse bite, specifically, fear of the sweating, vampiric death of rabies.

I was eight; this was our first year in a house. I had never in my life slept in a room alone. My parents showed me my room proudly, and small as it was, I couldn't imagine how I could survive in there, solo in the dark. Always my brother and I shared a room, or in the summer, me and my many cousins. My parents had bought me small furniture, sized more for a large doll than a child, and it was painted bright pink. The color reminded me of the inside of an ear. I hated it. As a child I hated many of the things I was supposed to love. My uncle gave me a real Patty Playpal doll, all three feet of her, for my fifth birthday. It stood large as me, looming, with pale, round, greedy eyes. I burst into tears.

GETTING TO KNOW

I often say I wished I had *gotten to know* my grandmother better while she was alive. And then my consciousness gets stuck on that phrase we use, so strenuous and yet so vague. You have to *get* somewhere in order to know someone, to find their foreign and somewhat random interior.

Standing by May and the spitting jam. Wild strawberries are so tiny even I at a small age recognize their tininess. And the dented, slightly shiny pot. I touch it uneasily. At the end of meals if we don't use paper plates—we generally don't— Helen and I have to fill this pot up and put it on the stove till the water grows hot, then wash dishes. With a large group we'll go through two or three pots of water and the process can take hours. If we had our way we'd just wash with the chilling, scumming water, but the women check on us and make us boil it fresh. Young as I am here in this jam story, an adult male will come to pour out the hot water for us while we step back, but then we'll have to wash till all's done, dried, bare again.

Wipe and scrape out the scraps of lettuce, sogged bread, fish tail from the sink.

After Helen in age comes Melinda, who's too fragile and fearful to be asked to do things. She turns the tide. The younger children will rarely get chores. No tides turned yet, though: My grandmother will hand me the pot at the end to wash, gelid with fruit.

The stove and oven in this kitchen are not much bigger than the Suzy Homemaker oven I have at home (the one that advertises it will help your little daughter remain socially a *square,* through its miming of domesticity, keep her from becoming one of the many hip wild chicks of the mid-1960s). The linoleum buckles and cracks. Everything beige, beige and old, with the stove's electric spiral cooktops, plastic knobs. Do other children stand in kitchens like this, threading around a grandmother, as even a small child must do in this space? Do they wash dishes for hours? Do they, to bring about the dishes, even have food to eat? With all the wary narcissism of a child, I can think of few alternatives to my own life. The world as I know it falls out of my head; what I can see and know are its horizons.

The wariness is partly that the given can change, and for no reasons I understand. My father tells me he works so he can *make money* and for many years I understand this to mean he goes to some indefinite place where he crafts coins and bills. He'll say he's trying for a new job and it will be a big move for the family, and I'll cry hidden under a piece of furniture, not sure why I cry at the word *move.* Or he'll get mad at my grandmother and say we won't spend holidays with her anymore, equally unthinkable. The terms of life at this age: You are portable, passive, stymied by the unimaginable alternatives to what you know.

So: This is the age at which I saw my grandmother the most, but making efforts on my part to know her better would be something I couldn't work toward even if I grasped the nature of it. I knew her probably better than her children did. I could have asked why she chose to make jam, sent me out with a washed coffee can and oversaw the hulling. I remember my grandmother said her own mother had made jam and she had grown up with wild strawberries in England.

Which makes me wonder where in consciousness, with its ignorant lags, its thing-making questions, does nostalgia come in? A sense that looks back, starts nothing physical moving, and doesn't ask yes-or-no questions. In fact, it undoes them, saying to the question of whether a time was happy, *Yes, it wasn't,* and *No, it was.*

HER RETURN

When my mother died in 2014 my grandmother began coming back to me. I looked through my mother's life—now closed, finis—and saw her mother's there: a dim form, a handprint at the end of the book. Ironically this return of my grandmother's spirit happened through physical things, through objects. I inherited stuff: first a lot of photographs, including pictures of my grandmother—a few sepia-toned shots of her as a child, most of her as a grown woman.

Some photos are black and white. A few are Polaroids. Barbour would see these in the spirit of *nows,* all still present, discrete, contained in their squares with the classic Polaroid smudge and thick white edges. The photos are glossy and date from that time when, if you wanted photos, you used a dedicated camera that did not answer phone calls or send messages, into which you wound film, catching it on a spool, then you unwound it when you'd covered it with images. You then took it to a drugstore or photo shop, to "develop." In a few days you went back and the person handed you an envelope of photos, among which would not be photos of yourself, unless someone else took them, though reversing the gaze of the camera would have been as possible then as now. No one yet had realized the one thing we want to capture is ourselves.

So we of the era before camera phones and selfies have envelopes full of photos of people who look mostly surprised at being photographed, as we collectively had to aim the camera somewhere. And this is true of my grandmother photos. She looks quizzical, bored, or perhaps a little annoyed in these pictures, most of which show her at the shore.

I also inherited the jewelry my mother kept, very little of it in her jewelry box, most of it stored in tiny boxes or fabric pouches hidden in her drawers, beneath underwear, or sometimes buried in used tissues. My mother had a phobia of burglary. My brother and I found most of her jewelry while emptying drawers and disposing of her clothes. My mother didn't really buy jewelry or much care for it, and her collection had pieces I assumed must have been my grandmother's before her—a very old cameo set in reddish gold, a few art deco pins, studded with tiny rhinestones and chunks of amber. These would not have been my mother's taste or era.

With her images and her ornaments came my grandmother. She has come like nostalgia itself, an itchy presence. She stakes claims: reminds me how much she really did matter to me. How she molded my thinking, opened in my mind a space of belief into which probably far too much can fit.

And how did she, who meant more to me in many ways than my mother, damage my mother, making room in her granddaughter for herself? This was not something my grandmother would do on purpose. I believe her sense of herself remained far removed from her family.

When I seek my grandmother through Jade the medium, she tells me to have a set time every day—say, ten o'clock in the morning—when I hold one of my grandmother's things in my hand and use a pen (she's firm about it being a pen) to do "automatic writing," as the medium calls it, on lined paper.

"She will tell you what to write," says Jade. "She'll speak to you."

And my grandmother, the medium says by implication, still observes the times of the day; even where she is, the stubbornly persistent illusion persists. She is trustworthy with a pen but not with a computer keyboard. And though as you'll see I've gone to excesses to find her she won't come to me alone, but will be drawn by the cameo or chunk of amber with strange silver horns growing out of the stone. I think of this medium's advice every day, though I have yet to take it.

-ALGIA

I was well into middle age before I saw that I've tried to build myself a Summer Land. I bought the house with the honeysuckle, half a mile from the sea. Bellingham Bay, not Barnegat Bay, but so close you could mishear in the gusts that blow off both waters. I put in fruit, I planted things—teal columbines with a whitecap of pleats; flowers I associated with my grandmother, like lupines and dusty miller. I wanted the blues and blue-greens, the low horizon purples of my childhood. Poppies, their red-sky-at-night colors drippy and saturated. We bought a house with a large shed or outbuilding and turned it into a work space, with a bed and a bathroom for guests. It's only two hundred square feet, but probably at that a bit larger than the little bungalow of my childhood.

I understood what I'd done when my father began referring to our place in the back as "your little bungalow." *Where's Bruce working, your little bungalow?* he'll say. *Where's your sister-in-law staying, your little bungalow?*

I had lived in my grandmother's Summer Land, where she swam nude, let her children raise themselves, escaped my grandfather for months each summer. When I had time to make my own Summer Land, I copied her. Which brings me back to nostalgia, the word—it translates from the Greek as an ache for home, literally, a *home ache*. But at any given time the place we live in is what we consider a home. Why are we aching for what we have? The word implies home is a thing always gone, and what we live in, a shadow, perhaps even a parody.

THE ART OF CONVERSATION

My Aunt Catherine, when my grandmother nettled her at the dinner table, would say, *And I thought you weren't allowed to drink, May?* and my grandmother only drank more wine and smiled to herself. It was a very particular smile she had, that meant she'd had this conversation very satisfactorily with herself.

THE LUMINIFEROUS ETHER

I was at this teenage time developing my relationship with my mind, my bipolarity. And it is a relationship, an intimate and attached one, the way you learn to get along with your heart. The heart will pound at times, and skip as if it's gotten tangled in its own jump rope. It will need some soothing, some relationship time. And you learn.

I can make no sense of the medical concept of an *episode* when a state of mind like my bipolar disorder "first occurred." Occurrence only speaks to visibility: like when that pale but grayish-blue of the veins seeps out as red. I was always bipolar.

It was, though, a state that struck the family and friends around me as an intruder, something that came from outside and lit into my body. Suddenly I said my heart might fly out of my chest. Suddenly I thought my family was poisoning me, and I refused to eat. It became more extreme when I stopped using drugs, in my twenties.

Andrew Jackson Davis has a rationale for madness. In one book he theorized that insanity comes from an excess of phosphorus in the brain. Maybe the idea floated around at the time; maybe Galen suggested it. While the man of good intellect will have two to two-and-a-half percent of his brain composed of phosphorus, says Davis, the madman will have four to four-and-a half percent (and in between lies the "eccentric," at three). Too little phosphorus means, in Davis's word, "imbecility." The thinking brain lit up with its phosphorus is a favorite Davis image. Perhaps the theory of quantum-ed phosphorus in the brain is right.

The element phosphorus in nature never exists in a free state. It must have a larger molecule to bind to. It's very flammable, and chemically is pyrophoric, meaning it can set fire to itself. The logic of it causing insanity is clever. It is one of the three elements used in fertilizer, along with potassium and nitrogen, and the reason fertilizer can launch homemade bombs.

In the dark, phosphorus glows, bluish-green, and can look strange, sickly, or beautiful (in the way of submerged, midnight things), depending. In photos it reminds me of Barnegat Bay and night sailing and the glowing bacteria vibrio.

I find this brain phosphorus theory in Davis's *A Stellar Key*. I feel this element: my radiating percentage, double normal. I have come to terms with being bipolar, and respect what it can do, the way I respect my heart with its irregular beat, the every-few-seconds failed skip rope. Still there are few things as grandly destructive as the brain immolating itself, every worldly connection scorching out—all things try to harm you, the wood patterns in the walls frown and creep. And part of you is outside the fire and wants to tell it to stop, but that wish too burns itself up. Like those trick birthday candles, lighting and relighting, while everyone waiting just grows tired.

THE BINDING PROBLEM

The story of my mother and the mouse bite has two sequels, each drawn from my feral days. Twice I overdosed, and she would not call an ambulance. The first time my brother called for help as she screamed at me for being in her and my father's room, where I had taken Quaaludes from my father's drawer and swallowed all of them. Then after screaming at me she left and made no effort to get help. The second time I told her I thought I'd overdosed (downs again) and she did nothing and for several days I slept it out. What she would have had happen to me these times, I do not know.

The first overdose I would not have survived without the hospital, and the second could have gone either way. I have never written of this before, my mother's three-time dice throw with my life. It's been too hard to think of my mother imagining me dead, or to picture just what happened in her imagination, another thing she liked to say she didn't indulge in much.

MY GRANDMOTHER AND
ANDREW JACKSON DAVIS IN HEAVEN,
KNOWN AS THE SUMMER LAND

Because the man known in life as Jackson has been here before. Because for him, it is a return, but the kind you make if, after years of vacationing in a town on the beach in another country—one with snorkeling and warm winters and caves where you lounge out low tides—you decide to move there. (This may seem a stereotype, but friends have done this.) You have retired. Your age makes this move sensible. The place feels familiar— the way sunlight bores through your half-closed lashes, the smell of it (which is never the same in any two places). Here, in this town, the odor is brine and the sweet vinegar of mangos mashed on the ground beneath their trees.

But your paradisiacal place is different when you're not leaving. The white sand, the smell of mango, are no longer like a postcard—a quick experience valued for its limits. A thing you live half for the moment, half for memory. They are now what *is*. Each vista would be subtly changed. You don't try to remember its beauties, but you try to forget them, so you can relive them the next day.

Are there tides in the Summer Land? Davis's sketches seem to say there are, though there are no moons.

Other things: The bushy foliage puffs out like clouds, in Davis's sketches. The Summer Land lies somewhere between Saturn and Jupiter, out in the Univercoelum, and stars are visible at night, though as I understand *The Stellar Key*, they aren't the stars we see on Earth. The brightest of these is named Guptarion.

My grandmother recognizes the Poughkeepsie prophet— his hair waterfalling back from his head and forth from his chin. (I assume his hair's black again.) My grandmother has read his autobiography and knows that he goes by the name Jackson.

Jackson, she says. *How nice to run into you.*

Have you been here long, he asks, *by yourself? Have you had a look around?*

The urge to explain still key to his character. Antidote to the strange feeling of being here for good.

My Louie came first, she says a little hesitantly, wondering if it's obvious she's not looking for him. Davis, who had three wives and left his second after thirty years, claiming his spirits told him to, sympathizes.

Rather than writing most of his books, Davis claims he publishes words he spoke while in a trance, taken down by a scribe. This, if true, would give Davis an ability to speak in long, scrolling, complex, compound sentences unparalleled in our world. In any case, here he's still a wordy man who seems incapable of not explaining and defining things. He guides May around, talking like the voice in his books.

You have been watched, he says, *by spirits. Always. No matter how many doors you have locked between yourself and the world.*

(This is not good news.)

He tells her about the eight hundred million tons a year of atomic emanations from earthly human bodies that create the Summer Land, constituting all she sees: *Therefore, these beautiful groves and vines and flowers, the soils, are constituted of particles that were once in human bodies!* May would note Davis expresses this in *tons*—the immaterial materiality in which she's wrapped. The puffy bushes grow in thick clusters.

Only in the Summer Land, Davis tells her, can someone be truly cosmopolitan.

All around her, she feels the water, the bushes, the hothouse brilliancies reshape at the emanation news: not the new landscape she reveled in, but a paradise made of the sheddings of people left alive, including her family—the new pretty-pretties made up of her old pretty-pretties. The particles she was always leaving. She must swim in them if she wants to swim, gather armfuls of them to arrange in a vase in her home, to indulge her old passion for roses. Some sort of atomic epithelial spray of hurts and griefs. And more than that, surely, but still. She is not my legacy; I am hers. And then, not to even be truly cosmopolitan. Is she beyond being bothered by these thoughts? Doubtful: She's only, as Davis says, "in another department in the great educational system of eternity."

In the end, impossible to resist filling the arms with those petals.

O rose, O pure contradiction, wrote the poet Rainer Maria Rilke, *desire to be no one's sleep, under so many lids.*

Whose lids? Whose sleep?

NO TAKE BACK

My brother and I as children were great lovers of the take back. Almost any comment could elicit that shriek of *Take it back!* which we amplified with smacks and kicks. One muttered insult roused more outrage than thieving from each other, or tattling. Chris and I said things that were ridiculous, things like *Your nose is full of snot.* Regardless of the true level of offense, we would demand our quantum past: The comment having been, by the offended one, noted, we insisted the offender perform the delayed-choice experiment, change history, take it back.

Both of us being equally stubborn about granting take backs—absolutely not, never, no matter how stupid it all was—we ended up fighting (over this and other things). Chris and I were fiercely attached to each other and fiercely combative.

Which drove our mother to tell us, pretty much daily, *Wait till your father gets home.* Then around 6 she'd greet our father at the door of our apartment, her face defensive with a whiff of spite. *Do you know what your children did today?* Of course he did not know what his children did today. It might be breaking one of the rules we broke all the time, like sneaking across the street to play in the cemetery. Or one of our many baroque awfulnesses, like the time we pulled bean sprouts out of can after can of chow mein, flicking them onto the kitchen wall where they stuck and made a Pollock of sprouts. Even wiped clean, the wall stayed freckled with the slick of it.

Or we might just have been hitting each other all day, doing what Chris called *duking it out.*

Often my mother would threaten to tell my father something, but at the last minute change her mind. We never knew which way she might go, which made my father's pulling up in his car at our apartment—something Chris and I watched for out the front window—another game. Like many games this one pleased with the adrenaline of the guess, the possible takedown. Could we push my mother to the brink, then win her back, with a *You look pretty,* a swipe of the dust rag? My father's punishments could be harsh—spending days in our room, sitting on the side of the bed, going without food. For this reason my mother weighed her options: whether the severity of his punishments, which could make her uncomfortable, would override her sense that we were out of control and needed something to make us afraid.

My mother's dead now and her past shreds away, quantum layers dissolving even more quickly than when she lived. I can see her face, though, in that small kitchen, staring at the sprouty wall, or at the hot iron on which I once, inexplicably, melted all my plastic Barbie shoes. A ruined iron, no ironing of my father's shirts and handkerchiefs. Bad news for all three of us.

My mother would look at us children and whatever we had done with a sad wonder. Sometimes you could see her eyes grow abstract with a look I'm sure I had myself at times with my son: *What does this mean for the future?* Will this child be forty years old and still be this, destroyer of walls and irons?

The eldest of four children, you'd think she'd be used to childish behavior, but she wasn't. Unlike my father, who when he had gotten tired of punishing sometimes favored *the talk,* my mother never asked why we'd done what we did. She asked what we were thinking, but always as a rhetorical question. My father would sit, his brows drawn into a thick mesh, and say, *Tell me* why *you did that.* To which we either answered truthfully—we had no idea—or made something up. *It was her idea,* my brother might say, and the whole mess would begin again. *Take that back!* I'd scream right into his face. *Take it back!*

To which he'd say, *No take backs.*

BRUCE AND ME IN SEDONA, KNOWN AS THE SUMMER LAND

I finish a stint of work in Santa Fe one summer, so Bruce and I rent a car and drive to another one of our psychic destinations, Sedona, Arizona. Sedona has the Hindu god Ganesh parked in a bluff of red rock, and vortexes that run energy fields either up your body or down your body. I never quite understand the difference. In any case, we find no Ganesh and no energy fields. There is a man chained to a tree, and there is a psychic who really appears psychic. The former is disturbing; the latter, surprising.

We found Mari the psychic (not her real name) in downtown Sedona, a place that calls itself the New Age capital of the US, and probably could call itself that for most of the world. It has, among other things, vortex sites. These are places identified during the Harmonic Convergence of 1986 as sites of spiritual energy. The Convergence marked an alignment of planets many New Agers claimed hadn't happened since the Mayan Empire (actually it was not that rare), and one that would usher in a new era of peace. The vortex designation, as I understand it, came about when an alien spacecraft was supposed to rise from a large formation named Bell Rock. A crowd came to watch it lift off. It never appeared, but the vortex title got applied to Bell Rock, kind of a metaphysical consolation prize.

Acquaintances of ours have moved to Sedona over the years. They've always been people who've renamed themselves, donning new names that, to my ear at least, resonate somewhere between hippie names and the names of Puritans, like Increase Mather or Praise-God Barebone. (I assume the Puritan resemblance is unintentional). There's Mineral Truth, Golden Allwishes. They don't so much "move" to Sedona as they get "called" to it. Sedona seems to have a PA system set to Bellingham.

Sedona is extraordinarily beautiful, a smallish town cupped in red rock. It looks as if someone chopped up pieces of the Grand Canyon, then set them around a valley. It is, I can't help thinking, far more beautiful than Davis's Summer Land, and if you believe the hype, just as loaded with spirits. The downtown has cosmetic shops; kiosk-sized businesses vending postcards and such; and shops selling crystals, psychic readings, aura readings, Reiki sessions, UFO and vortex tours, horoscopes, past-life regressions, chakra management, and many combinations of these. They have names like Center for the New Age and the Mystical Bazaar. All use the word *metaphysical,* which makes me wonder what my grandmother would think. I think, to give her credit, she would be sardonically amused.

Mari, our psychic, when we consult her, turns out to be a young woman with long hair, in a loose cotton dress. The other psychics I've seen have been surprisingly suburban. Mari would have looked at home at Woodstock. As I talk to her she gazes at some point across my right shoulder, *la-la-la*-ing to herself. She does this in a falsetto, like a coo you might make for a baby, or a signal to a dog to come in. Which I guess in either case could be related to her calling of spirits. After each stint of cooing, Mari stops suddenly and speaks. She barely looks at me and is not cold reading.

I tell her I want to contact my grandmother.

"I see her," Mari says after some *la*-ing. "The most important word to her was 'freedom.' She cared about her family but cared a lot more about traveling. And she had some kind of second sight." She did not pull out the bag of grandma clichés I'd become used to, and I was impressed.

The day before our psychic readings we took the Sedona vortex tour, which did not get our hopes up about the place. We scheduled the tour online, based on a recommendation from our Airbnb host. We imagined we'd be going with a small group, in a van, a 1960s van like the psychedelic van in *Scooby-Doo*. But the guide pulled up in a messy sedan, just us for the tour. The sedan had real estate brochures and magazines sliding across the seats. The guide was blond and conservatively dressed, but had a Mineral Truth-y kind of a name. I don't recall it, so I'll call her Bliss.

Bliss drove us outside of town, to various rock formations. At the first one, she led us in a two-minute guided meditation, exactly the kind a free app on my phone does, asking that we observe our breath and count. Vortex sites are supposed to heal you, and my feet and ankles crunched and ached from our Southwest hiking. I've broken, sprained, and had surgery on both feet and both ankles, and they always give me trouble. I fully expected this pain, against all reason, to get better: I imagined energy swirling around in my feet. Bliss rattled on about upward- and downward-flowing energies, Native American spirituality, which ratified that these sites were sacred, though it still took until 1986 for the Blisses of the world to identify them. Making this, I told Bruce later, the slowest co-opting of Native spirituality I've ever heard of.

Maybe Bliss sensed our disappointment. The vortex sites were pretty places, but no different than the red desert landscape around them. My ankles continued to crunch and ache, with the addition of an occasional little cactus spear as we walked around. I expect Bruce and I looked at each other woefully. Three hundred dollars for this? Bliss started handing us bottle after bottle of water, as if keeping us hydrated could justify the price.

Finally, Bliss said that vortexes move around, and anyway, we all have our own, don't we? Do we? I have no reason to think so. At one site she pointed out a rock face in the distance and asked if we noticed the Hindu god Ganesh looking down on us. She said the rock formation was clearly an elephant's head, revealing Ganesh's presence and spiritual energy. Bliss later showed us two rocks she claimed were a Native couple, a man and a woman whose story I forget. (These meanings attached to rocks, based on inscrutable resemblances, turned out to be a habit among Sedonans. Even at a Catholic church we visited, a caretaker showed us a Madonna-and-child rock, and a praying-hands rock. Which also just looked like rocks.)

Aside from Native Americans, Bliss drew a great amount of support for her New Age rants from modern physics. Physics has now proven, she said, everything she has told us. Plumes of energy abound and we are all interconnected and our spirits and bodies can be everywhere at once.

"Now we don't have to rely on the shamanic traditions," she said. "I mean, I love the shamanic traditions, but now we have the science, too."

The only notable thing we saw that day was a bearded man at one vortex site, a site that was a Buddhist stupa, or shrine. The man wore only a loincloth. It's not in this case cliché to call the man's tan copper-colored—his scrawny, sinewy body could have been cast out of molten pennies. He had long, sun-bleached hair, dry and wisping, and a braided beard. He'd chained himself to a tree by a hook through the septum of his nose. Not a nose-ring-sized hook: a large thick thing you could use to tie up a horse. He eyed us as we walked up the hill path leading to the stupa, but closed his eyes if anyone looked back.

So, the next day we head to Mari feeling like, beautiful as it is, Sedona's been a bust. I especially feel this way. I'm not sure what I expected, but something beyond the huge price tags put on enlightenment, the excuses when the spiritual seems to want to avoid you rather than find you, the co-opting of quantum theory to weave a fantasy of a malleable, immaterial human world.

Mari, and a dozen or so other psychics, work out of the upstairs of a New Age store, one that sells crystals and other minerals on the first floor. It has racks and racks of them, some twined into jewelry, some just in boxes.

We choose Mari based solely on Yelp reviews, which feels to us as unromantic as asking your Airbnb host for a mystical tour guide. The choices are bewildering—trance channelers, angel consultants, Ascended Master consultants, tarot readers, etc. We're stymied for an alternative to judgment-by-Yelp. Mari has not only the best reviews, but the best reviews in the area of accuracy, rather than easier-to-fudge qualities, like empathy, and "giving direction." She has five stars. Someone describes her accuracy as "uncanny."

Which it is. Mari tells me about my grandmother, and many other things that are not guessable. Aside from saying I'd like to hear from my grandmother, I tell her nothing, and ask her just to tell me what she sees. She says that my husband and I cut off money from a male member of our family, which we'd just, days ago, had to do with our son. It's upsetting, she says. We wonder how he'll do without our money.

Which is pretty much the theme of every conversation my husband and I have had in the last forty-eight hours. Mari mentions that Bruce and I once went together to a haunted place called the Hay House. This is hardly crucial to our lives, but true: We once went to a house of that name in Macon, Georgia. The guide told us it was haunted.

I wander through the store while Bruce gets his reading. He also finds his accurate, especially in the area of his father. Apparently now, unlike at Minister Jade's, his father Harold is ready to talk. I will just say that Bruce heard the terrible event happened when Harold was three, and naked in a bathroom with an older male relative. Of course we don't know if it's true, just detailed and believable.

While Bruce finds Harold somewhere in the space-time continuum, I find I can get crystals that do things like realign my chakra and my heart and my uterus. I see shungite, a Russian mineral that protects from the harmful rays of Wi-Fi signals and laptops, shungite being all over the place here, though the store has Wi-Fi, and plenty of salespeople tap furiously into their cell phones.

Finally, I buy a crystal necklace that has different colored stones falling like an ambling river. I spend almost $200, which is the most I've ever spent on jewelry. A slip of paper says the piece will bring out my beauty and my wisdom. As I loosen the chain from the plastic neck that holds it, I am ready to accept that. The reading with Mari leaves me caught up in a drunken bender of belief.

Later after the reading, though, I find myself feeling something else, a feeling I can only describe as soul-twinge. I relate this feeling to Rolf Landua's comment about the existential letdown of your theories proving right. Though I've leaned toward skepticism about psychic power, I did leave a little room for possibility. A door in this question closed, and I realized I'd been enjoying the breeze of having the door a little open.

Then, too, the reading had no predictive power, seeming more like straight telepathy. Mari just reached inside my head as if it lay on the table between us. She scooped it out. And while I felt excited that someone proved able to do this, it all sunk down into that place where on bad days I keep block universes, privileged observers, and zombies. Cool, for sure, but how does this change anything? I suppose I could have asked more predictive questions. I just found it all strange enough—this dipping together into the ice cream sundae of my brain—that I didn't think to.

Or perhaps I dismiss possibilities far too quickly, and my grandmother swooped down from the Summer Land, and she was there. And I'm a malcontent, mad when things don't work, disappointed when they do. *Oh, this is what it means to be in that type of a world?* It feels exactly like the old one.

GIRLIE: TO BEGIN

Her room had a pattern on the wood wall, like moss had spread there and been removed. The stains looked ancient, dark and fingered. *Goblins in the wood,* her mother told her little daughter whenever she noticed May staring at the wall. My great-grandmother did not smile or say she was joking. May understood, later, that her mother had not believed in the goblins but did believe in the virtues of scared children. Six was too many not to keep them all a little afraid.

"The goblins are at it again, painting the walls, Girlie, eh?" asked her mother.

"I don't believe in goblins."

"Ah, but they believe in *you.*" Her mother Louise put a hand on May's head in that way that could have been affection but also had a pressure, a *Don't move* in the tips of the fingers.

Actually, May believed in goblins but had convinced herself they looked like dogs, like friendly Pomeranians whose paws scrabbled in the wood.

May played with a pair of elbow-length gloves her mother had given her to distract her, white and kidskin and tiny enough that when the child buttoned them up they snugged her arm. May would never be tall but had a robust body and would never be as petite as her mother, a fact her mother realized with satisfaction.

Nor would May be a beauty, but she had something other-worldly about her looks; oval face, a nose prominent but not in the least Roman: wider. It was, her mother thought, that the child never looked surprised. If you told her the turn of the century was coming, as it was this year and as she had in fact told her, if you told her she'd soon have a little brother or sister, it passed across her face as if you simply confirmed what she'd already discovered on her own. Louise could barely picture the child's eyes widening.

RECREATIONAL HIDING

My grandmother and my grandfather did not share a bedroom (a pattern repeated by my parents), except at the shore. They never had, as far as I know. Their rooms at home were not even adjacent, but my grandfather had an odd little bedroom at a turn in the stairs of their house in Fanwood, New Jersey, a town my grandmother called *a good address* and that my parents would move to also, later in life. My grandfather died in this room and I'm not even sure when my grandmother realized he was gone.

My grandmother's room, at the top of the stairs, had a vanity table with skirts you could fold out, stapled to two arms of wood that tucked under the tabletop. The vanity made a lovely hiding place and I have a vivid memory of hiding in there as a young child after I had broken something, some thing I thought was valuable. I hid there to avoid punishment but no one ever looked for me, and I found the absence of interest in my whereabouts far more terrifying than punishment, and crawled out after a while crying and shouting.

We lived in a two-bedroom apartment then. I was never alone at home and couldn't have found a spot where no one could see me. And so I practiced recreational hiding. To be alone but not in the dark, with the sounds of familiar people around you—this to me was the most soothing thing there was.

My grandmother's room smelled of talc and lilac and lavender. It reeked of stuff you put on your body to come between it and the depredations of the physical world, its sweats and its bloods and its agings. Her closet was different. She had furs—a fox that had the head and the long paws still attached, a coat ringed with raccoon at the collar—and mothballs, and the closet hit you with that sharp odor of pelt and a sting of ammonia. Something once alive was in there; also something meant to eradicate the evidence of living. It always felt odd to me that my grandmother, who was fond of animals, would wear fur, but she'd had these coats for a long time. This odor came rushing to me when my aunt and my mother told the story of the man who lived next to them with the skunk skins nailed to an outer wall. I knew the smell of that side of his house, could even imagine he, unmoored as he was, might have found it comforting.

When the family got together, we children were herded into my grandparents' basement, which smelled like mold and had a huge loom where my grandmother wove rugs. We were expected to stay there. I believe I was the only child who'd wait for a chance to sneak up to my grandmother's room and prowl: for the scent of powdery lilac, the gold brush and comb on the vanity table. A pink lipstick, though my grandmother did not use makeup as a rule. A stretch hiding under the vanity skirts, enclosed like a fox kit in its den, hearing kids yelling, adults arguing, a rattling of glasses, though in my hiding place I wasn't implicated in the sounds. Then the closet, the whiff of cleaned but potent skinned animal.

Perhaps this is why my grandmother confided in me. She noticed how I probed for evidence of what her life consisted of. I hid like a stowaway under the mirrored vanity table, even threw the fox around my neck, its hanging paws tracing my ribs, under my chin that triangular face with eyes sewn shut, a creature that should have died and decomposed decades ago still tangible.

Anyway, to practice recreational hiding only works if people are around you, if they wonder about you. Under the vanity I was a quantum particle hovering before the slits.

1899

Girlie stays awake for the change of the century. Her father slips her champagne, which tastes like sour cider and tickles the within-part of her nose. Her parents' neighbors have come over. She understands the day is very important. Her father has been reading aloud from the paper, full of words that ping around in her head: The bloody Americans have shifted the *pig iron* market in London. The Prince of Wales has been to a county meeting in Norwich, and he has *dragoons*. She sees hard sculpted pigs, nothing like the raucous stained creatures she has to feed once a day, fiery soldiers, perhaps with wings.

The century, a solid thing made of time, is turning over. When it does it becomes fresh and new, with wonders escaping from its body—carriages pulling themselves, human voices carrying across the ocean, and much, much more that no one can begin to imagine. Her mother has told her so. The neighbor Tom toasts for a century of peace.

The century arrives on this day an old man and turns to a babe again, the newspapers say.

"This will be your century," her father has said to her several times in the past week. Now he extends his non-champagne-holding hand to her, open-palmed, as if giving her her hundred years of time.

"To 1900!" the adults say, and drink. Outside she can hear the pigs snuffling in their muck, not bothered about the bloody Americans (*capitalists,* the newspaper said, meaning, she is not sure what), who may not care about that type of pig at all.

BOXILLS AND BINARIES

My grandmother and my grandfather set a paradigm for the rest of the family. Half of us travel constantly, travel like those pursued, while half of us will never leave our homes. Helen and I call it the Boxills who go and the Boxills who stay. She is the latter; I am the former. She has only flown two or three times, the latest (fifteen years ago) to see me, and only after long phone consultations on liquids and Baggies rules and pat downs and luggage sizes. I once took a long weekend to travel from Bellingham to Hong Kong. My husband and I cut back on travel some while raising our son, but we have itchy feet.

Like my grandmother we travel with or without money, which often leads to staying in strange marginal situations, once a studio in an Italian town so tiny that when the Murphy bed came down there was nothing left. Or a suspiciously cheap place we rented outside of Rome, owned by a man who did performance art by dressing up as a Minotaur and roller skating while setting himself on fire. We had to flee the flaming Minotaur because he turned out to be as bizarre as his act implies. He lived next to an Etruscan necropolis and had stolen an enormous amount of ancient statuary—grave goods—from it, a place called Veio. I'm sure his theft broke many laws, but for the few days we spent in his house, we shared it with charming long feet, hands, and heads with round fat curls and the cat-like Etruscan smile.

The man, Paolo, had promised to leave when we arrived but he didn't, and clearly psychically could not, and followed us around yelling we were landing on the stone stairs too hard, we were touching the counters the wrong way, we did not wipe the water out of the tub soon enough after leaving it. He also seemed to have rented his place to a number of people at the same time.

To which Helen or Mark, another stayer, would say, *Why the hell pay money to have that happen?* and we goers would say, *It's an adventure.* By which we mean, I think, scratch life and make it bleed a little and you know you're here. And they'd answer, *But you are here,* and *Why not leave it alone?*

PART III

THE TERRIBLE UNLIKELIHOOD

It's also true that Constructor Theory has at its core the idea that anything that is not impossible (i.e. forbidden by the laws of physics) has to be attainable somehow—so unless one has a clear law forbidding something from happening, one should try to realize it.

—Oxford physicist Chiara Marletto

MY WORLD

It occurs to me as I assemble these old conversations that I didn't believe the world as I found it came to exist until I came to exist. The past as narrated to me seemed improbably different. It resembled the inexplicable whatnot preceding the big bang, or a parallel universe, a thing radically different. I got this thinking from listening to family stories, and to what I learned through the endless town crier called television. It was not ego; I believed my world could have existed before me, but it didn't seem that it had.

In first grade my teachers, weeping and clutching transistor radios, led us kids into a gym, then forgot us as we grew restless and began to shove and mutter. Our president had been shot and died as they listened. Such assassinations, my family said, did not happen. Then as I watched TV I saw the man who shot him get shot in turn—wince, clutch stomach, and fall. The man, Lee Harvey Oswald, wore a pullover sweater and looked small and young. When police brought Oswald out to answer press questions, some makeup person had filled his brows in thick with an eyebrow pencil. It seemed an effort to make him look older, more capable of shooting a hole through history.

This death of Oswald, swift, televised, was a thing that did not happen either. More shootings followed, including of college students by the National Guard. A murder rate that climbed up and up and seemed to anoint many different groups, each in its own way: the groups that killed for politics, the men who simply wanted to hurt women. The Manson Family. Even the bomb, that began before me but came into its final shape during my early years, seemed part of me, not of anything that came before. That level of destruction had been birthed like me out of the '40s and the '50s and it changed the world.

In this other, mythic universe that predated me, men who had a yen to would climb into your room at night, staring at you in your sleep. This was acceptable and led to no further action on any side. If you wanted a house near water, you grabbed some land and built one. For drinking water, you dug a well. If you wanted soda, you sent children out to dig roots. The business of your life did not have to have an existence in the realm of postal systems and other official noticers unless you chose it to, which probably you wouldn't. The thieves who broke into your home would clean after themselves—more or less—leave and come again, but never touch you.

This was not a pleasant thought, about the world and my position in it as one who coincidentally slid out into an altered worldscape, though it's a thought I've heard echoed by many people my age. I didn't feel my birth itself had changed things, but that I had happened to come to be on one side of a divide too yawning to close or traverse. And it felt branded or shamed, to have landed on this side of it. Maybe to be no better than you ought to be. On my side, there was no such thing as *just strange*.

WOULD IT MATTER IF I SAID IT DID?

"What did she mean by that, Jesus was a scientist?"

My mother and I are sitting in her living room in Fanwood, New Jersey, in the house where my parents live, when I ask this question. They moved here after I left for college, partly at the urging of my mother, who also craved its *good address.* Though it's an undistinguished, middle-income, New Jersey town.

The house will be one of the torments of my parents' age but they're proud of it, its 1960s design with areas separated by slight stairs, and its working fireplace. The stairs will prove their undoing.

If they meet friends of mine my parents will mention where they live and often say I grew up there. This is not lying. It is something they do, a continuous translation of the past into the terms of the present moment. Everything that's happened shifts as it passes through the new life and its filters. It is our lives as an endless feedback loop, a co-creation: a flotsam thing that only needs to be compatible with the present. I have learned to be afraid of this translation. I'm not sure whether I do it myself.

My mother has not yet developed the memory loss that will define her last years, as it did her mother's.

"She meant Jesus was a scientist."

My mother and I excel in these tautological questions and answers.

"When did you realize you weren't a Christian Scientist?"

"Well, it didn't really make any sense," my mother said uneasily, "did it?"

EVEN A MAN

When I turned eight my parents bought their first house—a small one, in a blue-collar town—and we moved in and I learned that people secretly want to kill those they love.

It happened this way: Suddenly, with a living room housing a TV and other rooms in which people could and would stay for stretches of time, I fell madly in love with television. I came home from school every day and switched on our RCA set, looking for monster movies. I loved vampires and were-wolves particularly, but I watched everything, creatures from black lagoons, ants the size of trucks, slimy Things that could squish into the room through a vent and engulf you. I learned who would win in whatever epic combinations these creatures fought, whether it was Frankenstein against Dracula or Godzilla versus Mothra.

And I learned what a common human enterprise it is to want to kill those you love. The werewolf instinctively tries to kill the person it loves best, explains the werewolf expert in *The Wolf Man* (and every other werewolf movie), noting how lycanthropy exposes our bestial side, a side of all of us that waits for a chance to set on its beloveds and maul them. When *Dark Shadows* entered my life two years after our move, the witch Angelique cursed Barnabas the vampire with death to any woman he favored. Even the man-fly of *The Fly* tried to harm his wife with his fly arm, with only his puny human arm to save her. To keep himself from killing her, he had to get her to kill him. The Invisible Man drove his father to suicide. The Creature from the Black Lagoon tried to drag beautiful Kay into the muck. No loved ones, it seemed, escaped. Later this would put a strange light on my mother and her willingness to let me die.

These films and their characters were my own spirit guides, though of course I had my skepticism: I did not really believe that even a man who was pure in heart and said his prayers by night might become a wolf when the wolfsbane bloomed and the autumn moon was bright. But I saw how the material of the body could change, whether through a bite or through radiation and its mutating gigantisms.

The witch on *Dark Shadows* came from Martinique. That island lay near Barbados, and my grandfather's sister had moved there as a bride, and been poisoned to death by her Catholic mother-in-law, who could not accept a Protestant daughter. This I had heard from my grandmother.

And in my viewing I saw the other sides of the other sides of human nature: the gentle sadness of the wolfman when he is not the wolf.

"That child is glued to the television set," my mother complained on the phone to her sisters. My father said I *wasted all my time on the idiot screen.* They both allowed me to, however. Did any parents feel they could affect a child's development in the 1960s? Hippie parents on communes, maybe. My parents parented like everyone else did, at least everyone we knew—as if your children were formed things dealt out to you, the throws of some otherworldly deck of cards.

The night before we moved into our house, and I began my education in monstrosity and love, my brother and I spent the night with an old aunt and uncle of my father's. My parents wanted us out of the way while they packed and moved stuff out of our apartment. I remember almost nothing about that house except that it had a taxidermied owl in flight at the bottom of the stairs—wings out, claws out, as if coming in for a landing. It was really a very large owl and it too had that odor of animal skin.

And each of the movies I loved had its expert—its Dr. Van Helsing, its Dr. Yogami—the character who arrives after the mysterious death with the key to the mystery, the one with the vague European accent that smacked of occult knowledge, the one who always sounded more like my grandmother than like anyone I actually knew.

COMMAND

My father's main complaint about my grandmother, aside from the WASP thing, was that she controlled my mother. He complained bitterly about this. In this he resembled my grandmother, in that he would not have told anyone but me these things. He claimed that everything from their wedding's details and date, scheduled during my mother's menstrual period, to where they lived and how they raised their children, was dominated by my grandmother and her wishes. He was not wrong. My mother's one rebellion was leaving Christian Science, and my grandmother seemed indifferent to whether her children upheld her truth or not, perhaps even smug about their dismissal of it. My grandmother wielded a sway over my repressed and quiet mother that was hard to understand, especially in a relationship so clearly not based in love. My mother called her mother every day or two and got off the phone with orders—they had to spend Christmas with my grandmother, though my father had promised it to his sister Philomena; I had to re-enroll in Brownie Scouts; I must have Louise as a middle name.

I could only think of my mother and her mother's relationship in terms of the B movies I loved or *Dark Shadows,* the show with the absurdly redundant name. Angelique, the witch, controlled Barnabas; Barnabas controlled Ben Stokes and Willy Loomis. No love anywhere in the story, or none that lasted. There's a control that comes with one fierce, feral, personality overriding another.

My mother and I had a distant relationship, lacking in any touch or words that I would identify as love, though every now and then she would look at me and snap out an order ("You go and lose weight now," or, "You go and get Bruce to give you that ironing he's doing"). Her face—that sudden and so unfamiliar look of command—almost made me sad for her, though of course I didn't listen.

ANGELO-ANDREW

In my mother's relationship with her mother, and in her life, there's a mystery I still know little about: her first fiancé, a man born Angelo Guglielmo, though he anglicized his name to Andrew Williams. He, like my father, was Italian American and an accountant (my father too Anglicized his name, from Nicola to Nicholas).

I know about Angelo-Andrew through a few discrete moments: once overhearing my father and mother arguing about her keeping his ring; my grandmother's story of telling my mother about his death; and a lunch I had with my mother, alone, in Italy, where we'd all gone to meet up with my father's family of sharecroppers in Campania. I don't recall where everyone else on that trip had gotten to, or even what city we were in, but we were alone and drinking wine, and my mother, suddenly voluble by her terms, told me she'd been engaged to a man who'd died in the war. And that she guessed Italian American men were her "type," a surprising admission, since she'd spent much of my life complaining about my father's Italianness: the food, the Catholicism, the body-drenched humor.

She once, to my husband's memory, mentioned Angelo-Andrew around us both, in my father's presence, at dinner, just mentioning he'd existed and had like my father been Italian American and an accountant, and that he'd died in the war. Wine was also present here. My mother generally would not talk about Angelo-Andrew, avoiding the subject even more than that of illness. After her death, my father claimed to have forgotten she'd been engaged before.

After my mother's death, my brother and I found, buried in the used-Kleenex depths of a lower drawer of her dresser, a bracelet Angelo-Andrew had given her. It was a silver chain link bracelet that seemed meant to resemble a dog tag, and it had "Andrew Williams" and his Army number on one side; "I love you Mary" on the other. It shone like new and the ten-dollar price tag still hung off it (this would be nearly two hundred in today's dollars). My mother, true to her form in life, had saved but never worn it. We used his service number to find a copy of his death certificate on the web. We could not find any other information. The death certificate told us he'd served in the Army's 6th Armored Infantry Division and died on August 24 of 1944, so he would have been part of Operation Dragoon, liberating southern France. His body was shipped back to the States and signed for by a Joanne Williams, and he was buried at Holy Sepulchre Cemetery in Newark with a bronze marker.

The only other thing I learned from that death certificate had to do with the war itself, not Angelo-Andrew; the rush of the clerk who filled it out was palpable, a man sitting with a pile of too many deaths to record. The words dashed and slipping between the lines, everything possible abbreviated, even Armored (*Arm'd*) and Infantry (*Inf*). When my father and I visited my mother's safe-deposit box after her death to retrieve her wedding ring, I found her first ring, white gold with a square-cut diamond, hidden under the cotton in the same box. I do not wear the bracelet—I can't bring myself to cut off the price tag—but I do wear the diamond from time to time. And wonder how it felt for my mother when the ring passed from one meaning to another, still with that stone's bright lit inwardness.

My mother only referred to her late fiancé as *Angelo,* though she did mention that he'd changed his name.

He came from Newark. I can imagine how my grand-mother felt about him, and how she might have announced the news of his death. I cannot imagine if my mother might have been a different, more stubborn, more May-like woman with Angelo at her side. The years between his death and her 1953 marriage, she lived in her mother's home.

My mother had said at our lunch that if it weren't for the war, I would have had a different father. I wouldn't have existed, I told her, and found it touching that she hadn't looked at it that way.

ENTANGLED PARTICLES:
MY FATHER AND MY DIFFERENT FATHER

Entangled particles, as I've said, function like mirror twins. One cannot be altered without the other changing too, regardless of the distance between them, which could be so vast that information traveling at the speed of light would take ten thousand years to reach the entangled partner. This distance doesn't matter—the change will be instantaneous. Einstein dismissed this possibility, but particles have been entangled, and gone on to behave in sync, again and again in controlled experiments.

My father came from Brooklyn and changed his name. My different father came from Newark and changed his name. Both sat at desks tapping on those adding machines of the 1940s, the ones that spat out a narrow row of numbers, and calculators, very like the ones Einstein and Bohr would have used. Both went into a jewelry store and asked to look at rings, indicating with a lateral palm and perhaps a pinkie my tiny mother and her tiny fingers. Though from my point of view I am the moral of the story, neither of them thought about me at all.

As my father became a widower perhaps a man rose and found a woman, in the Summer Land.

SPOOKY ACTION

Mary tries to learn to call her husband Andy, or Andrew, not Angelo, the husband's name when she met him. Sometimes, as she'll do with her children later, she mashes his name together: *And-Angelo.* He is back from the war, whole and gotten on with a local accounting house. She has married in 1945, at the age of twenty-five, moved out of her parents' house. She owns one diamond ring and a dog tag bracelet she wears every day on her right wrist. The sight of her mother does not fill her with the clamp-toothed, damp-rag-in-the-stomach feeling she'd get if she had to stay longer.

Her mother has never given her terrible news over a wet dish, handed to her to dry. She still has to learn to make tomato sauce, but from her husband's mother, not having to learn from his sister Philomena because her sickly mother-in-law died before her eldest son married. Mary is young and not tired of anything yet and doesn't mind the learning. She looks at magazines, figures out how to apply makeup, knows she's considered pretty. Though when her children come out looking like Andrew she doesn't mind, doesn't imagine another item on the list of things life could do for her crossed out.

TRYING BELIEF

When it comes to my grandmother's vision of the world, I have wanted to believe. I tried again recently, though my old faith that this could be possible is gone. I'd tripped in my garden and yanked my foot right at the ankle, a spot where, two years ago, I'd broken it. That spot, still sensitive, hurt so much after the fall that I couldn't walk without putting back on the foot brace I'd worn for months while the old break healed.

I couldn't stand the thought of another year of limping. So I sat down on the couch and closed my eyes and did what my grandmother taught me: visualized my perfect and immaculate body that had nothing in it that could be shattered or even strained. I pictured feet with no bones in them hovering a little above the earth. I told the nerves transmitting the pain signal that they had no reality. I added a little AJ Davis and imagined little spirits everywhere. Healing, I told myself, is a possible transformation, right now, under the laws of physics. I did this until I could almost believe I could believe, until my body seemed to have dissolved into a robe of thought.

Then I rose to my feet and the pain bit back at me, my foot telling me it is muscle and bone and nerve, and while it may report to the brain it cares not at all what changes that brain has conjured up. The brain is no master and commander but more like an operator at an old-fashioned switchboard: Put the messages through and you can daydream about any reality you want.

THE MAGNETIC SLEEP

One night in June of 1966 I am nine years old and dying again, in that way that happens at night in the dark, a place where nothing seems as vulnerable as a lone consciousness. It may be one in the morning. That many nights like this have passed and I lived through them doesn't signify. Each night has its own set of rules; all children know this. A mosquito has chosen my ear for its whinging and when I can't get rid of it I lure it to the bathroom by turning on lights. I smash, bloodsmudge it. This mosquito has the blood she needs to fertilize her eggs and shouldn't need more, but here she is. She's been dive-bombing my ear for half an hour, making my near death all the more undignified. That she has her blood and still dives at me shows the difference between facts and life, life so much less neat.

The bathroom run is the only way to ditch perseverant mosquitoes, but to get there you have to pass the back door, its panes teeming with the sense of lives in the darkness, hints of strange movement. We are often the only lit house for miles, though cars drive all night to the bulkhead at the street's end just beyond our house, slowing, turning. The bay slaps at the bulkhead in that way of waves smashing against a wall. They sound tired, as if they'd like to stop crashing there, but they can't.

Sometimes cars inexplicably stop. There are mud men and boys who wave turtles like fanged swords, and God-knows-what crawling out of the nuclear power plant and an actual lagoon just ten feet behind us, crisscrossed rows of black water lashed in grass. I can imagine spiny creatures crawling out of them, looking for girls to submerge.

My grandmother lies in the room by mine, asleep. She would tell me that I cannot die, that my body—spirit materialized into a phantom of form—cannot be destroyed, only transported, the way in the morning I'll throw a bag and myself in the car and get out at my family's house in northern New Jersey. I am not body really but all mind. But this doesn't signify either.

My grandmother has spent the day sharing with me her metaphysics. She has said, as she so often did, that if God allowed sickness and death that God is not good, and we know God is good, don't we? I feel assured of no such thing. God I would say is a jury-rigger just like us.

My little cousin Melinda cried all afternoon because she thought she was going to die of typhoid, and Mark would die of it too, because the pipes under the house have burst (again) and sewage is flowing, and Mark crawled in to take a look. Melinda will actually die at fifty of an epileptic seizure—a bipolar medication thing, she went on and off meds so much her brain began misfiring. The first of us cousins to go. Right now though we've pacified her and gotten her to sleep.

I don't worry about the typhoid but I do think I may die at the fangs of berbalangs, mythical creatures from Filipino culture with heads that detach from their body and fly on wings, looking for the entrails of living humans to eat. Helen read me a story from her new copy of *Ripley's Believe It or Not!* magazine. It ended by saying berbalangs had left the Philippines and been spotted flying across the ocean to the United States. Helen read me this and showed me their picture; fanged, winged, human heads. Then she rolled over and fell instantly to sleep. This is how Helen sleeps—a rollover and a cliff-deep drop. If Helen thought she was going to die—which she does not—she would still want to sleep first. That's the difference between us.

When a lot of adults stay at the shore we girls get kicked out of the bunk bed room and onto the front screened porch, on couches that have mildew farther down even than the springs. The odor is strong and deep. These nights I never sleep. I feel exposed; I might as well be lying in the street, gravel pocking my shoulders. I can feel the knives or gunshots about to rip through the screen, or the berbalang heads, hovering. Cars prowl and stop and doors crash open.

Melinda fusses wherever we put her, particularly about disease, and she knew about things like cholera as a tiny girl. My aunt Millie often makes Helen and me go to bed with Melinda and pretend to sleep to keep her quiet, which we resent mightily as ruining our fun—Melinda often won't sleep, and we're not allowed to leave until she does—but our mothers won't interfere. It is kind of a rule among the adults that the kids are available to use as you see fit.

The shore, where I beg to go, is the only place I'm afraid to this degree, though I'm afraid sometimes at home too. Looking back I can't explain the fear and it makes no sense: just three months before this berbalang night, a man murdered Wendy Sue Wolin in Elizabeth. I worry about this and other such things more at the shore, though my entrails are probably much safer in Holly Park than at home.

At the shore I'm surrounded by other people, and here their proximity only ups my fears, in the same way my grandmother's optimism deepens my pessimism. Not only can these others not protect me, but their presence is part of the lure, the strange little houses in my mind appearing to the monsters out there like the single bright bulb in the bathroom to the mosquito. I can't share my grandmother's faith in my body's immunity, its ability in the face of danger to shimmer immaterially away. My failure serves as another beacon. I am as permeable as the things I am always killing, slitting the bellies of; or peeling off their backs and limbs.

NO MATTER

"So therefore when we each arrive in the Summer Lands we shall find persons who are perfectly acquainted with all that we have ever done; no matter how multitudinous the doors, how thick the walls, or how many doors were locked between us and the world."

So when my grandmother came to the Summer Land on her death in 1985, she found herself, as AJ Davis tells her, with those who knew all there was to know of her, a position she'd never been in before. It's not clear in *A Stellar Key* how these witnesses functioned; were some in the Summer Land dedicated to watching? Assigned to you? Did they find you and introduce themselves when you got there?

There's a great deal in Davis, and his idol Emanuel Swedenborg, of what we'd call the stalker: the spirit as stalker. In this my grandmother would not be getting what she wanted from the afterlife. I believe she brought back so little from her trips because she did not want us to be able to imagine them—to pierce through what she coveted or what she handled to the stuff of her days—just as she wanted to be free of us when overseas. It must have felt like living two lives.

However it came about, these watchers witnessed how May handled climbing stairs in a whorehouse next to an exhausted prostitute (the half-mast eyes, the rouge!), May murmuring a decorous hello, as she would feel she should. They'd seen the woman I would guess claimed to be widowed long before she was, as *single* sounded undesirable and *married* made her sound no better than she ought to be. They'd witnessed her tell about her four children, or none, whatever came to her at the moment; watched her eat sheep guts packed in sheep stomach and try cow's blood from a glass; been privy to her seasickness; to the strangers who *ahhhh*ed over her story about England, the place she prided herself on once it no longer surrounded her.

As soon as my grandmother grasped the handle of her trunk and walked out the door, her stories freshened. She could talk about Mrs. Eddy and the world that was good and the matter spiritualized that is the body. These Summer Landers know this May as well as the one we knew. As Davis writes, they see through her locked doors. And this makes me sad, though my grandmother's drive that I learn about her also baffled me. Now I am sorry. I wish I were more often the one who watched.

BACK DOOR

A woman I knew some years ago, when I had a young child, lost her husband. She had young children too, which is how I knew her. Her husband was around forty and had contracted a cancer of the blood. The cancer didn't kill him, though; he was responding to treatment when the stem cell treatment killed him, dying "on the table," as people say in these circumstances, though at no point would a hospital put a patient on an actual table, as if he were the main course.

I sent the woman a card and some food and ran into her after the death at a children's get-together. All the mothers gathered around her, murmuring.

"I just can't believe it," she said. "I keep expecting him to show up at the back door."

I did not know this woman well, but I've heard that phrase many times since, people who've lost someone expecting the dead person to appear, often after a sudden loss, at the back door. Why the back door? What have these dead, who aim to skulk rather than step forthrightly back into our lives, realized?

"I turn around to the back door," she said, "and I just expect to see him."

AS GOOD AS ANY

In my early life most of the religious teaching I got was from my grandmother, though I went to Catholic churches with my Aunt Philomena and Uncle Vito and my cousins, their four children. That family, the Giordanos, were never clear in their theology and my Catholicism could have been its own *Ripley's Believe It or Not!*: the blood that would run down your chin if you took the host after what my cousins called "a bad confession"; votive candles lit with prayers that could not be refused if you were in a new church; priests mumbling wafers not just into flesh but into bloody flesh. The doily my aunt grabbed off a table and popped on my head because she'd run out of chapel veils and "Girls, youse cover the head!" as her accent had it. The crown of my head versus this scrap that had just sat under a casserole dish—God, a hard guy to figure, opted for the latter.

My grandmother at least had internal consistency: a good God who is also Love; no flesh; no illness. Not even death in the sense we understand it. Your mind and its connection to Divine Mind keep you always. Have faith, ask for the right understanding, and it's yours.

On this year's anniversary of the death of my mother, my grandmother's faith works for me as well as any theory of how this mighty improbability continues. I mean not healing but life, not just my mother's or mine or yours but anyone's—my cat taught me to sit on a particular part of the couch, where he can both sag his body down to rest on my shoulder and look out the window, mostly surveying the birds. He sits up when a chickadee gets close, and his tail winds around my neck. Friend loves me absurdly, and loves to hunt birds. Or did. He's old now, and mostly just likes to imagine it, putting his phi to work.

Friend also manages to do many things—teach me where to sit; wash with a paw his gray nicked ear; kill a young varied thrush; even maintain his 101 degree internal temperature. He does it all without in a matter of hours decaying.

On this death date the achievement seems remarkable, and whatever you do with your life does, this little coin pressed in your hand.

HER PRACTICE

That my grandmother did not to my knowledge pray, ever, that she seemed unlike her heroine Mary Baker Eddy to have spent very little time thinking about God, the great Mother-Father, or Jesus—*Jesus was a scientist* was all I can remember her saying about him—forms a part of this story I've avoided. It's challenging; I don't know what it means. People may have called Eddy deluded, but no one could deny her rectitude, her retired, abstemious life devoted to the Mother Church. Eddy shunned mind-altering substances and even mind-altering practices, and trying hypnotism—something my grandmother and Uncle Joe used to play around with, waving a pocket watch in front of our eyes—could get you excommunicated from her church.

My grandmother went to the Christian Science Reading Room once or twice a week. This opens the possibility that there also existed a Reading Room May, a woman who by her own declaration to her peers there would never touch a glass of wine or a manhattan or a gin and tonic or—a drink that took over my family for one summer—a piña colada. But the days when I picked her up she seemed to be chatting, telling stories, or bragging about her grandsons. She went to services but not regularly. She seemed to love her bout with opium, a drug Mary Baker Eddy took once just to prove she could will herself to resist its effects.

That I spent so much of each summer with my grandmother in a small place would imply that I understood her spiritual practice, but I saw no signs of it other than her avoidance of medicine. I suspect her faith lay mostly in the infinite extension of her own life and her power over the body, over the universe in fact, a reality she saw as malleable and radically subjective. But it's quite possible her spirituality existed like the self she took on her trips—there was a May that existed in prayer, in regular reflection on God and the Trinity—and she simply brought nothing from it back for us.

BACK DOOR II

The dead are casual when they return. They do not want to bother. Knowing how they'd stand out, they try to slip back. They're afraid the old space won't open; they try sneaking in. They may not speak any longer. They understand the truth of timelessness, maybe, but know that we don't. Perhaps they remember the history of the back door, for service people,

deliveries, those of little consequence. They mean to be unob-
trusive if they can. Maybe they wish to feel useful.

And who answers the door for them, who tells them there's
ground clinging, and nothing to wipe it away?

THE START OF THE REST OF THE STORY

The pond is hardly swimmable. A murky, mucky, slurping bottom, and little room. May hangs her bathing costume under
cover of an osier branch, a thick green broth of leaves. G who
brought her there has hung a shirt, downward, white arms
stretched, as if someone from the crown of the tree is falling,
stretching arms to the earth, never quite achieving it. A vision
of gravity suspended. May in the water, G windmilling a back
stroke, tight circles for them both. They splash one another,
swim side strokes with their hands planing through floating
leaves.

The osier and its leaf-roil becomes a room, framed by the
gravitylessness of G's shirt and its own atmosphere of suspen-
sion, light greened by leaves mimicking stained glass. What
might they do together? What might they not do? Their bodies, the way a point of pleasure both rushes them into time and
then holds them a while, out of it.

PART IV

SMITHEREENS

I attempt not a likeness but a resemblance.

—Artist Alberto Giacometti

BARELY A GAME

My brother Chris and my cousin Mark, as kids, had a game called Remains. It never really began and it never really ended. They called it "playing Remains" though it was more like something that just happened, a thought experiment maybe, than a chosen play. Remains barely met the minimum qualifications for gamehood. But yet.

The background of the game was this. Chris and Mark battled for hours with their green plastic Army men and other things they had in miniature, like tanks and cannons.

Chris—and Helen and me if we joined—played as the Allied powers in World War II, and Mark insisted on the Axis: the Japanese and Germans. Mark knew specific battles and the boys chose swells in the land and positions accordingly. Mark would label spots things like "the Sudetenland" and the "Maginot Line." He hurled invisible grenades at us and shot us with twigs he called *panzers,* though we had only a dim idea of what that meant. Both sides took prisoners but our side had to take Mark's word for it on what his weapons did, a fact we regarded with some suspicion, as we generally lost.

Anyway, the boys played War outside more often than in and would lose their men. And they'd leave them behind, even through the lathering black squalls we got. I think everyone my age remembers those soldiers: green, a couple of inches high, in various combat positions. They might stand or kneel with a rifle; advance, an arm cocked, waving the soldiers behind to come on. Seams showing the cast of the plastic, in the uniforms of World War II. Really a boring toy—small, plain, nothing in it you could manipulate, the way you'd pose a Barbie—but still their favorite. I think the boys loved the soldiers' disposability, along with the volume their cheapness lent itself to, and the way in their cast stances the soldiers gazed and gestured toward one another. Barbie seemed to need us, while the soldiers had their own world.

Anyway, over the course of the summer the soldiers and their gear got left and lost, and then Mark or Chris would be outside, coming in from a swim or something, and notice poking from the soil the tip of a bayonet or butt of a rifle. The one who saw evidence had to shriek the other's name and also shriek the word "Remains!"

So we would randomly hear "Mark! Remains!" or "Chris! Remains!" Then together they dug the whatever-it-was out. I think sometimes they deliberately buried their soldiers, then let them slip from their minds.

The accidental discovery and the digging was the whole thing, which is why I say Remains pushes the definition of "game" a bit far. Or perhaps Remains makes sense if you think of time and weather and dumb luck and a kind of perversity (you stub your toe on the bayonet speared by a figure wearing the uniform your father almost died in, just a decade or so back) as the other players.

THAT MODERNITY

"It will be 1900!" her mother told her. "Who knows what will happen! We have boats that go under the water! People talking across an ocean! A carriage that rides itself without a horse!"

Over there in that America they are doing these things, she says. They are clever.

May's mother Louise was sweeping out the bedroom her daughters May and Marjorie shared, and chatting with May in the overenthusiastic voice the child drew out of her. Baby Katherine still slept in her room.

May watched Louise with those light eyes as she swept. "Then will the horses die out, Mummy?"

Louise met her daughter's look. "What?"

"If we don't need them," May said, "then the horses will die out."

She had a rocking horse in her room, made of wood, with a mane and tail made from the hair of a real horse. Its eyes were larger than a real horse's and had so much white in them the thing looked frightened, an expression that went comically with the frantic rocking of the children.

"No one will let horses die," Louise told her.

"They kill them in battle," May insisted, "with their guns and their knives. Who knows how they got Archer's hair?" And she pointed to the rocking horse.

Louise's daughter liked to bring up death, and for a five-year-old, almost philosophically. It was like May to think not just about *one* horse dying but about *all* the horses dying. Once when Dot had scarlet fever May cried because she said the whole family would get it and die now, and then of course so would their ginger cat, Belle, because there would be no one left to feed her.

"Someone would take on Belle," Louise told her, ignoring the rest.

"Perhaps a kitten they would, not a full-grown cat, and not a ginger, they're common," May told her, and Louise changed the subject.

"However will you get on in this life," she said.

SMITHEREENS

If the bayonet tip or gun muzzle poking from the ground happened to lead to a disembodied arm or weapon, the boys would
dig it out and say, "It's been smashed to smithereens." We threw
firecrackers onto leaf piles, or sometimes little bombs we made
by scraping hundreds of match tips into tinfoil—one matchstick left out, as a fuse—and we'd burn them to smithereens.
Both boys as entertainment would suddenly turn on lights at
night to Raid the mosquitoes, poisoning them to smithereens.
Things we heard about in Vietnam, napalm or Agent Orange
or bombing campaigns like Operation Rolling Thunder, blew
villages and people to smithereens. If I mentioned cremation
to my cousin and my brother they would have said, *Oh right
Susie, burn you to smithereens!* Smithereens, a direct opposition
to the Summer Land—that calm step from one existence to
another almost identical one. Smithereens too was a place that
existed, in our minds and in the world, and once there things
did not reassemble.

PLAYING

As with Remains or U.N.C.L.E., when I talk of playing War, I
feel the word *play* needs a qualification.

In a sense: It was a game, and talk of playing War would
leave any of the four of us cousins knowing what to do, how
to set up, though the boys played War more than Helen and
I did. But it would be truer to say we lived war in a way that
made the playing of it a kind of running commentary or endless speculation.

We had Vietnam and its television presence, unparalleled
in any war before or since—flagged coffins, Vietnamese girls
dusted with napalm, a photo of a man (bullet finding head)

at the instant of execution. Vietnam dragged on, escalated, became Laos, Cambodia. And it was tragic and pointless, and both Mark and Chris knew they could face the draft. Mark did, in fact, get drafted, though he never left the States.

But behind 'Nam stood the hulking presences of the First and Second World Wars. World War I belonging to our grandfather, World War II to our fathers. They called it *the big war* and talked about it incessantly: the U-boats in the big war, the children in Japan asking for a chocolate bar in the big war. It seemed unlikely that this current war, spreading through Asia, would simply end. We gave ourselves fifteen years until the next world war once again ate through every fourth or fifth teenage boy. And with the existence of the atomic bomb, this new war would eventually cease choosing individuals and decide to end cities, parts of countries flapping off in chunks. Niels Bohr had modeled the atom right before World War I broke out. With World War II came the Manhattan Project, men in the desert working out how to split places like Manhattan to pieces, cratering, cancering. The atom, rendered to its timeless constituent parts, left the world of clock time with a mushroom-shaped hole in it.

World wars were part of the planet as it unfolded for us, as was destruction on a level no one before the atomic bomb could have foreseen. I wonder now at how strange it must have been for my parents and grandparents, having to take in this possibility.

Most people alive thought as we did. Of course we would keep going to the moon and soon vacation there, as we'd cure all communicable disease. Of course there would be a third world war and some country would deploy the hydrogen bomb, the atomic's new fierce incarnation. My generation's rejection of getting older than thirty may have been a psychological preemptive strike.

President Kennedy had urged Americans in 1961 to build basement bomb shelters, and many did. At school we had what we called *air raid drills,* and we filed into the basement or just crouched under our desks to practice evading the inevitable bomb, teachers reminding us to keep identification on ourselves, our version of Remains, our practice for the fact of Smithereens.

SAW

Her cap falls into her eyes. She has blankets from the donation pile, boiled for bandages. She leans forward, cutting one up—an old chenille—and jerking her cap out of her eyes. Her pinafore is bloody, streaks and smears and the prints of her hands, fingers splayed and colored like a child's drawing. She has given the man his ether and chloroform through a mask. There's no knowing how much to give: enough to keep him moving a little so they can tell he's not dead, and not enough to still him completely. There's no sparing him the agony.

She's irrigated with Dakin solution the bloody mouth, snagtoothed with bone bits, above the man's knee. Dakin is her antiseptic, the latest, a replacement for the old iodine. It leads to less putrefaction, but it's unstable, and they're always running out. In this case it's hopeless; it took transport too long. The wound putrefies. The odor's physical in the air: rancid fat, the egg you've smashed and forgotten gone sulfurous in the back of the chicken coop, and most unfair, a tinge of sweet. The doctor now balances a saw on the man's thigh. The man screams *NO* and then a confusing chorus of women's names, perhaps Lily? Sadie? And, inexplicably, the word *bread.* The man clutches her hand, the one she wiped to a red ghost on the pinafore.

She keeps pouring in the Dakin. Antibiotics several decades away.

The doctor confuses her by addressing her as *Girlie,* her family nickname, though it's just what he calls all the nurses. His dark hair holds a part like a line of white thread. She focuses on this as he works the saw. The nurses are afraid of him and he does seem to hate them, but she sees into him, how he's young and came to this when he still felt he had power, power mostly located in his hands. He had learned to do clever things with them. He felt things like blood and patients could be taught to behave. But: hot jets, unpredictable, both.

She thinks, half watching the amputation, of Lady Jane Grey, coerced onto the British throne, then executed at the age of seventeen. The spectators could not believe how the neck gushed, how much blood this young girl had in her. Now the doctor's hands loll in the mess, and trash cans hold human limbs because probably they can't save those limbs, and their decisions must be made instantly. They had been promised a quick war. A few bad decisions, not thousands of them. Instead *quick* only applies to the way they practice. She's just left a man whose face—without its attachment to a neck she's not sure she would have known to call it that—has bulged and pumiced with mustard gas. He'll be blind. She can't help him, so she directs the nurses to tend the others first.

How has she come to terms with it? Because she has, she realizes, though she's not that much older than Lady Jane, who died with, aside from volume, dignity. It has to do with the feeling of her own body, its tucked-in pleasures; of her body in water; she has been swimming with her friend G in the pond lately without her costume on. Sometimes in the water their bodies touch, and sometimes when they climb out it feels natural to connect again at those places where the body seems to ask a question or suggest a need. *We expect children not to figure out the obvious* says G, self-touching.

The hangman, a Jack who ministered to many trades, wielded an axe. He was both the opposite of the nurses and, in some ways, their peer, in that disposal, disposal was everything. First before the blow he asked Lady Jane for her forgiveness. As they did back then.

IF A LADY HAD NOT FORGIVEN

There are always these moments on which the mind snags: knots in the current where a feather catches. What havoc that could have created! With such a clear sense of the next world, and little faith these decisions on traitors were the right ones. Lady Jane had as much royal blood as the queen at the time, Bloody Mary. Only her pardon potentially between the hangman and damnation. The crowd gathered and eager—it's a spectacle, someone guides her blindfolded head to the right spot on the block, all must come off as planned—while the hangman leans confounded on his ax. If Jane were to close her lips and refuse absolution. Yet it never happened, not once. May supposes the chance of torture, and what seemed like that time's remarkable concern for what would be said about a person after death, outweighed the drive to keep existing, even for a few minutes more. It kept the condemned in a forgiving mood.

PLAYING CATEGORIES

May has her categories in her nursing: the Stumps, the Pulled Taffies, the Cyclopses, the Want-No-Eyes, the Grunts and Gaspers, with gas-gangrene in the lungs. She uses the words to herself. You could call it a game, she thinks. Some men fit in more than one category. The game sorts and orders. Makes her feel there are places in the world for the men. The first man she called Cyclops really earned it; an eye had been blown toward the center of his face. She imagines him on an island, in a cave, hungering for Ulysses. Unlike their parents, she and her siblings like to read. She brings inner stories with her, to fold around everything, like Christmas paper. Or maybe butcher paper.

And the one who lost his leg the day before. He's half delirious, half asleep, rolling and reaching his hand for the knee that was, now air in a blanket, but he scratches away at it with his dirty and snaggled fingernails. He begins with a small scratch from his forefinger but within a few seconds he's working all five fingers furiously. The itch, she knows, is unbearable. Though nothing is there. It will get better, but not entirely. And if they took his other leg that too would become a present-and-absent leg, as real as any—scratched, rubbed, rolled around—when covered by a sheet. How much of him, she wonders, could disappear?

Her sister Katherine, her favorite sister, died last year against the cab of a lorry. She died at seventeen riding her motorcycle, which she did in skirts and sometimes in trousers, with sunglasses like a pilot's. She'd fancied herself a New Woman. She took May in the sidecar, tires spewing gravel as they roared up to her barrack laughing. Men stared, and she realized there was power in being a woman who could make a secret of her laughter's reasons. Then her sister died, and sometimes May feels she works in a museum of Katherines: the gashes, the skewed limbs, the smashed cheeks. The sight of a patient will hit with a sudden shock, a miming of her sister's concluding face and body. But the men are mostly hanging on, reaching for their absent-presences in their sleep. If you die, she knows, you lose the game entirely.

A NEW GAME

Meanwhile, back in 1905, when May was ten and nursing her dolls—who bled not at all and whose limbs could generally be reattached—Albert Einstein slipped into a chair at the patent office and came up with the theory of special relativity. Of course he came up with it over many months. Einstein was young then, with neat, dark hair. He considered patents for things like electromagnetic clocks, as he dismantled science's concept of the force they measured.

Special relativity holds that physics laws are constant for all the universe and there's a set speed of light, which fact dictates that time and space must be not absolute but relative. An astronaut moving faster than earth moves would age more slowly than a man on earth, a concept known as time dilation. If time dilation didn't work, your GPS wouldn't work either, as just one of many proofs. The instrument's calibrated to Einsteinian time.

Max Planck in 1900 identified quanta. And in 1913, three years before my grandmother assisted in that surgery, Niels Bohr modeled the atom. In doing so he revealed the yawning nothingness out of which everything, including we humans, are made. If the atom were a football field, he wrote, the nucleus would be a football on the field, and the electrons would be a swarm of gnats buzzing above the outer tiers of seats. What we perceive as solidity, in a substance like steel, is just strong magnetic force. Our reality is timelessness and void, though for the soldier with the putrefying gash in his leg, all of that incredible nothingness of his body meets this one cleft above the knee, and this one void is all that matters.

At the time of this surgery, in 1915, an Einstein who'd shed the patent office figured out that space and time warp and curve, and gravity warps them. The math for this theory, general relativity, took him ten years. It proves that massive objects cause distortions in space-time. This is now familiar, as when we sent the Viking spacecraft to Mars and watched signals coming back to us get bent in time and space by the pull of the sun. We were used to this; we planned for it. Time and space became for Einstein his "stubbornly persistent illusions."

If you read popular books explaining the theories of relativity, the authors will try to explain Einstein using the analogy of trains: one man on a fast train unable to calculate the speed of a man on a slow train, and so on. The Einsteinian trains simply held men in time—or men caught in one version of time—to make a point, and not the men the trains of 1916 actually carried, bloody, yipping in their sleep, torn, gashed limbs and pumiced faces. Heading for my grandmother, for whom what was relative was the ability to sedate them or sterilize their wounds.

When World War I began, doctors and nurses still used products and techniques dating back to the 1840s. Surgery had been a fairly dormant field, though they learned as they went. Still, though, a true antibiotic—penicillin—lay far off, 1928 for discovery, 1942 for first use. Many of the men my grandmother treated died of suppurating wounds; no one could reach into the illusion of the future to pull out a decent antibiotic, or even a decent anesthetic. At the start of the war, my grandmother would have attempted to numb her surgical patients with cocaine.

These men of my grandmother's were caught in their own relative space-time: the time they lucklessly fell into, relative to the Great War; their space its theater. Their need for one science, medicine, to be advancing by leaps, relative to physics, another.

There was reporting of the theory of relativity back then, though I'm not sure if my grandmother would have heard such stories, or understood them. It was an extraordinary concept to release into that mid-war year's hell: space and time as relative, bendable. Time like ripples in a pond, or the air echoing back from a bullet. I expect it seemed like science playing a very bad practical joke.

LOUIS

He is small, pale, skinny. He is down a finger and has a bullet nudging his carotid artery. A British doctor said, "We operate," and if they had, she knows, the man would have died. An American doctor said, "Leave the bullet there, it's too close," and added "it'll give him iron," very much an American kind of humor. The patient opted for the opinion of the American doctor. Though he is, at the moment (she doesn't know how momentary this will be), no longer British as he was by birth, or American as he will be, but Canadian. She respects him for his stoicism, for being one of the few patients who isn't constantly crying for more medicine, more procedures.

She finds herself drawn to his eyes, pale blue, but housed in large heavy-lidded round orbits, Spanish or South American looking. He has a faraway look, and his eyes seem sent from far away. He has full lips. He watches her quietly as she goes around the ward. He's always quiet but it isn't shell shock; he doesn't jump or yelp in his sleep. When he sleeps she watches him. His face's many allegiances are striking.

Everyone by now knows his story. He comes from somewhere in the West Indies and joined the war as a Canadian soldier. His connection to Canada isn't clear; his mother lived for a short time in Thunder Bay, Ontario, and Louis once served as a cook at a Canadian lumber camp. He won't say much more. One day he tells her the lumbermen threatened every day or so to murder him. *They'd say, We'd kill you if you were big enough to be worth the trouble.* He finds this grim but funny. It's true, he is a small man. The only story he's willing to tell about Canada feels like a poor recommendation to fight for its flag.

Louis lost his finger as he combed his hair in a foxhole: *bing bing* and gone. Though probably his fingers and the comb deflected the shot away from his head. Then he gets reassigned as a clerk and in his job handling paperwork for soldiers coming and going, he falsifies his records, erasing the fact that he has already served and been wounded.

He files the faked papers and has himself shipped back to the front. This time again the bullets buzz for his head and one lands in the neck, nicking the pulsing carotid but leaving it whole. *The luckiest and probably stupidest bastard who ever lived,* the doctor said.

The *why* of it of course absorbs them all. They get men caught fleeing, shot by their officers in the thigh as they run, rope wound around their legs jumping off boats, in spite of the many dawn executions for desertion. Who goes back??? No one from this world, she thinks.

Why? She asks him.

I was sending men every day to their death, he answers, *and I couldn't do that to them without doing it to myself.*

But of course, he could; that was the whole point of living. Luck came your way and you grabbed it, even if in holding it you lost a few fingers. The answer makes her impatient.

Anyway she doesn't believe he means it. He says it with practice, without his Bajan singsong. His loathing of the front is real: an acid churns inside him. He had a Belgian man executed (perhaps shooting the man himself? It isn't clear) when a windmill moved the wrong way in the wind. Signals to the German troops. *Bloody cowardly Belgian bastard,* he hates them all, along with, now, Canadians, British doctors.

She has not known any soldier to do what he did, but she has seen a wistfulness sometimes in the returned: They want to tell her about the front, how strange to be where death and life are all that's real, to the point that you smell them both, waking to sleep. The moments separating then joining them. Where a man can stand then dissolve to blood in air.

STAKES

There was so much at stake. They tended to say this when they healed, looking ahead to a life without those stakes, maybe selling something, like notions or shirts, no one would die without. Or a life with the stakes less tangible. She could not even see her menstrual blood anymore, from the first chocolate-colored smear to the spurt, without conclusions. If it came while she nursed she took a bandage for herself, a blanket scrap. She changed in the privy and carried her bloody bandage with the men's used bandages, washing what she could, burning the rest. The head nurse, looking at what she carried, would nod, not knowing one bandage, like the key to a riddle, held a different story from the rest in her arms.

May bled more heavily than her sisters, and some days she felt flowing on her legs, a twitch inside like a stitch pulling, then a flood. It worried her, but each time on the day it ended she loved her body, how cleverly it knew to stop.

MAPS AND BAYONETS

Recently I was with a group of my cousins and my brother and we were drinking wine and I threw out the story of the man who stared at my mother and her sister in their sleep. To my surprise, they all remembered the story. The consensus among them was that in those days (this would have been the 1920s or early 1930s) people didn't worry about such things. Maybe I have to accept this answer, though my rational mind asks, why not? Children were vulnerable then. People understood sexual assault even if they didn't name it. And murder was murder and death was death.

I have had a lifelong memory of my grandfather sharing with us children (Mark, Chris, and me, maybe Helen), more than once, a bloody jacket, a soldier's jacket he wore when he was shot in the finger. It turned out—via agreement on the part of everyone there except me—that what he showed us was actually a map, a map of southern France, with blood smeared over its geographies. My cousins had seen the bloody map more than once and said someone in the family still had it, though we couldn't recall who.

My grandfather had been holding the map open in front of him when shot. He brought it out to show us along with his uniform and I had conflated the two, but it's an odor memory for me more than a visual one, of the copper smell of blood. And an imagination memory, having had to picture all that blood spurting out of one rather small person (nosebleeds being my upper limit at that age).

Louis, my grandfather, was very silent and didn't interact with his grandchildren much, except for these few urgent proofs of his history. My cousin Diana in the middle of this conversation went out and came back with a bayonet which my grandfather had gifted Mark when Mark was five years old. It had, my grandfather claimed, been the bayonet he fought with in the war. We noticed examining the bayonet that it was made in France and dated back to the late 1800s, so it must have been a hand-me-down weapon.

The bayonet was heavy and very sharp, clasped in a scabbard, grayed like old tin, and given its age and history, it must have killed someone, or multiple someones. Still it had been a gift for a five-year-old (not to be taken and held by his parents, but for him to use), a little boy who must have had trouble lifting it, though he'd go on to become obsessed with playing war. Mark had just brought it to Diana's house to share it with her adult sons.

It seemed my grandfather had taken upon himself death education. It was a thing he pressed on us physically in blood and sword, and in his stories, of windmill traitors, of the trench where he slept on a dead body. Finalities, openings, end points. Maybe he worried about his wife's teachings, of death as a small shift in our manifestation as beings. The map strikes me now as a likelier vehicle of this education than a jacket. Its promise of a rational place and then the overwriting of its fields and roads with a roundish, rust-colored, and new cartography.

SIMON

At this same gathering Mark's daughter Tara mentioned to us that, like us, she had slept as a child in that bunk bed bedroom next to the blue Simon-table. One night, she said, it moved itself across the floor as she lay in bed. She wasn't asleep and heard the scraping and saw the table push itself, ending about half a foot from the wall. It scraped a few times and her mother Beth came in and told her to cut out shoving the table, and go to sleep. She told her mother it wasn't her but the table moving itself, and her mother left in high dudgeon, after which the table shoved itself back into place.

HERE BULLET

After dealing with her one-hundredth or three-hundredth or one-thousandth bullet, May begins to see only them. They become her mission, her patients, her fetish objects. She has to trench the flesh around each one, a pit slowly deepening under her knife so she can tug the invader out. As the whole lique-fies. Then she drags the slug out, with a kinder wrenching than she'd give an infant being born. The man himself, his body, has become container. It hosts what cannot stay but often cannot easily be removed. Because from its first life as assailant, the bullet becomes plug. Unless it lands right in the brain or cen-

tral gut or heart or lung and causes death (and she rarely sees
these wounds), the bullet often holds the flows back and kills
on removal: a nick or nudge into a vein or artery or organ, a
small pull then a defeated and finalizing gush.

She's begun to save them. They take on so many shapes:
a shiny clay sculpted by the body's resistances. Compacted in
tight folds, like a sleeve pushed up an arm. Or resembling the
top inch of a finger—a groove on one side, slope on the other,
striations almost like a joint. Or caved in, twisted metal peeling back. The most unusual she shoves into a headache powder
box. Later, the box will cross the Atlantic with her, a remem-
brance of a time without time for remembering. She feels that
rush each time she opens the box: dig yank, dig yank. The outcome could be anything, the body moved to a bed or to a pile
of other bodies. This was all you were left with.

MATRIMONY

At my grandfather's cot in the makeshift hospital, my grandmother holds his left hand—the one with all five fingers—as
they say their vows. He has used what-money-she-doesn't-know
to pay for her small diamond. The vicar puts the question to
her roughly and she says *Yessss*. She tried to back out but now
becomes slowly glad. The word in her head is *New*. New York.
New England. New Jersey. Like where she comes from, but
reinvented.

May slips her diamond back on her finger as she walks
the gangplank of the Royal George, hundreds of them chan-
neled onto the small island. She has kept the ring up till now
in her little purse. The giant statue with the torch has a calm
beauty, though it's French. He will be somewhere near, looking
for her, accompanied by the mother who is still beautiful after
fourteen children, and whose accent May never fully under-

stands. If he misses her and she goes out alone into this stream of humanity, she thinks. What then, what couldn't she do?

Or she says yes in a small Episcopal church in Westfield, New Jersey. His deep-set eyes never look at the cross or the altar. Her hand at her belly, though she keeps willing it away.

FIRST

First the blood dries up, the messy spurt her mother said would guarantee a hearty child. Then she feels somehow different, full, down there. In the third month she pictures the thing, so little, and then it's slipsliding around, like a key turning over and over again in a lock. A quickened minnow, rehearsing the darts of escape without escaping. Then it becomes a weight, a doorstop shifting. July arrives, hot and the hospital bed heavy with her sweat. Her first American Fourth of July, and the fireworks that made her husband crawl fearful into bed, that for her opened the darkness into bright, giddy, plunging stars.

When she meets the doorstop five days later, it has become a little girl. Colored pink, blood, and white, a crier. May is back at the war. But this wounded can't be passed on. She has taken a man with her from the war but here's another body, and the field lies inside of her, and the trenches, and the enemy.

In two years, the child will develop an astonishing temper, tantrums that would *make the Front look calm,* her husband will say.

SPONGE

Once as a girl May overheard her mother talking to her aunt—her mother's sister—about pregnancy, the two women in the parlor eating piece after piece of sponge cake, May at the door;

she wanted to tattle on her brother Eddie, who said he would feed Felicity, her bride doll, to the pigs.

"The terrible thing about pregnancy," her mother was saying, "is the body learns what it can get away with." She sighed that the cake had gone stale. May, who wasn't sure of the meaning of *pregnancy* but knew it had to do with her existence, crept back to her room.

May remembered this comment after she gave birth: a human moving its head and feet and arms inside her for almost a year, plunking itself on her bladder; the pee leaking out; the months of gas and farts and drops tearing from her breasts. No travel. Then labor with its pain that felt like nothing could be worse, followed by the yes-there-can pain of the baby crowning—midwives called it *the ring of fire*. And the thing itself, waxy and bloody and looking like a creature that had lived its life, died terribly and already begun to decompose.

Nothing had disturbed her spirit-body the way the presence of another one inside of it had. It hadn't shaken her beliefs, but it did make it seem suspiciously as if spirit was a thing allergic to itself.

RAPUNZEL, RAPUNZEL

My mother before my life had very long hair—thigh-sweep-long, Rapunzel-long—so long she had to ask others to comb and braid it for her: her sisters would, or my grandmother, or early in their marriage, my father. Though she disliked fussing over her children, my grandmother insisted my mother keep her hair long and got mad when my mother after my brother was born had it cut. My mother did this secretly, as she went to doctors, though my father knew. She was an exhausted young mother and had postpartum depression, as my father told me. But her mother only responded to the hair, to the breach of her orders. Only my mother had long hair in her family and my grandmother acted as if something magical might climb up through it one day.

RAVISHED

So May comes knocking.

What have I thought her into, dressing her, making her talk and move.

Presenting her, as she would put it, as *no better than she ought to be.* Though she loved to think of herself as naughty, transgressive, and she might under her scolding approve of that. All this to the woman who gave my mind its freedom to move thought into the realm of what exists. I know for me she never left her private Summer Land, the place where she led the keenest part of her life, at least the keenest part that occurred around her family. She lived her restlessness there, she infused the brines of her body with the brines of the sea. And she persisted. Simon lived on in the side table and he held her, his skyey, thick skin reflecting her, like the drunken spirits summoned by the drunk medium.

Then in 2012 Hurricane Sandy slicked the place away, in the case of the Little Bungalow, neatly, foundation only left. The house floated down nearby Potter's Creek, collapsing each day further into itself, but on the foundation slab a jar of pennies—collected by my Uncle Joe, dead at the time of Sandy—stood. The house rapt; the penny jar left, not a crack in the glass. And a sledgehammer next to it. *Here it is,* the hurricane seemed to say, *I would not take your money.* Or the destructive force I do not myself need.

Sandy crashed the Big Bungalow onto its side. The surge filled the house four feet up, ripping apart the furniture and floor but leaving even little papers, grocery lists and calendar pages, intact above. My cousin hired a man who shoved the house back onto its cement blocks, though it staggered still, unwieldy, a strange kneeling like a camel's. Too warped to enter, the house held a yellow *Condemned* notice.

The storm surge came from the back—the lagoons—and drove stuff from the Big Bungalow into mud piles, like archeological middens, in the front. My brother and I went to look and dug through those middens, many months after the storm, and found pages of the books on shipwrecks and plane crashes, brass Monopoly pieces, like a boot and an iron, from my mother's childhood Monopoly set, the one we children also used. I pocketed all I could, even forks and spoons. Chris said, *We're playing Remains.*

I calculated with what things I pulled from the mud how many times my grandmother might have touched them: a thousand times, for the deep-bowled spoons. More than that for the bride doll, ceramic and very old, its squashily real face and high Victorian gown, a childhood doll (blown apart at the waist) of my grandmother's.

A THINGAMAJIG

My parents' house in Fanwood, their last house and the one I never lived in, is painted an achy green, and though small, has many levels. The stairs are a problem; both my parents have fallen and broken things: hips, ankles, backs. The house abuts power lines. People think these lines cause cancer, so my parents worry no one will ever buy the house, though anyway they won't move, won't go somewhere where it's easier for old people to live. The neighbors, Tom and Mary, died a decade ago in a murder-suicide, on my son's birthday. Mary, as my mother Mary did, had broken a hip, and her husband chose not to cope with it. He was in his eighties, she in her seventies. One newspaper ran my parents' address by mistake as the site of the deaths. Throughout that day, my father told me, cars pulled up and strangers left lavish sheaves of flowers at his door, as people do at the site of tragedy. My father brought the flowers next door, to the right stoop, though the place was empty and remained empty.

My parents have been robbed in a home invasion though they weren't quite sure what was happening till it was over. The men got into the house with fake badges and led my parents into the basement. My father saw one man stealing and one hiding in the bushes outside. *Of course,* people tell me when I complain they won't leave, *it's their house.* Meaning, something of the Summer Land adheres to it.

CONUNDRUMS

My father and my mother had places on the couch, where they sat most of the day with a paper or puzzle between them. My father still has his place, and I tend more and more to sit at the same end of my couch in my own home. I wonder when I'll be unable to sit anywhere else, capable, of course, but restless, eyes shifting around the room, until I move back to my spot.

Things lose their essence at my parents' house. Nothing is itself, for my mother when she lived, and for my father. The stuff of life reforms itself into *thingamajigs, whoziwhats-ers, whatsits, watchamacallits.* I can't tell you how urgent these words can become. My father also has had a lifelong genius for malaprops. He will rave about the evils of giving out *conon-drums* in the schools, and you will have to attend to grasp that it's not puzzles (slightly mispronounced) but condoms that infuriate him. He will ask you how your *chapstick* is doing, for *chapbook,* back when the two of you could still talk about writing. His microwave morphs into a *Microsoft.* None of this is an age thing; he's always done it to the same degree. It's sur-real and requires an adept listening—he hates to be misunder-stood—but I admire the way he finds language so plastic, and so his own. He is Giulio Tononi. Language is not good enough to explain this.

I have no name, often, at my parents' house, but I have utility. My hands are capable of glasses of water, making food. Sometimes I'm known as *Chrisusbrujimar* or *chrisusbrujinick.*

ALL THE FAULT OF THE ZOMBIES

My father has always had a strange way of sharing this kind of news, of Tom and Mary, for instance (and I should admit in all honesty I know Tom's name—I saw him often—but don't remember his wife's. It's my memory that's made her Mary and I can't shake that, though I could find out her real name eas-ily enough). The deaths occurred on my son's birthday, and my father called to say he needed to tell me something terri-ble, but wouldn't until later, because it would ruin (*roon* in his Brooklynese) my son's birthday. That call came on a Saturday.

I spent the weekend imagining more and more awful sce-narios, then called Monday and heard the story. Tom shot his wife and then himself. Tom who had fished for bluefish, and brought fish all summer to my mother, chunked, skin-on in icy Baggies. My mother had me defrost and cook it when I vis-ited—she found it too strong, and I developed a workable fish stew recipe, which had tarragon, I recall. I still see Tom at their back door, and when I think of the shooting I can't put a gun in his hand: just a clear bag of dark-fleshed fish. He had bad children, my father said, or he would never have done what he did.

We had a little excitement last night. This my father calls and tells me a few years ago. The son of the man across the street, who lives with his father, shot six rounds from a rifle at the neighbor's house. The police came and had a scuffle, took the son away.

Why did he shoot? I want to know, and my father says, *He has long hair and tattoos, you know, all over, like.* The shooting makes the New Jersey newspapers and I look up the story, though there's no more information than what my father told me; less actually, as the man's long hair and tattoos don't make the paper. I think of my parents' house at this time as the center of a triangle, poised between three points, power lines on the left, murder-suicide on the right, gunfire in front. It's mystical, as triangles are: Greek. They're caught in some field made by voltage and violence, one that sizzles on the edges but holds them static within. Although they're at their *good address.*

ADDICTION

Was not a word anyone used in that separate Earth I once inhabited, the one that existed at the side of normal people on the street (with whom our contact was often begging money), where addicts actually lived. I've since met older addicts who use that term, generally after rehab stints or jail. We did not. Heroin addicts were either looking to score and sick, or shot up and well. Meth users taking the drug in long stints of days or weeks—which was common—were on a "mission." I don't recall a term for afterward or before.

In *Mental Disorders,* Andrew Jackson Davis describes the "yellow-eyed, the hurrying and fluttering opium-eaters." I did not know yellow-eyed or fluttering addicts, but I did know junkies and tweakers who loved chess—many more players than you'd find in the general population—and who could stare at the board with an unmoving profundity and then strike suddenly at a knight or a queen. They were quite skilled.

I knew people who shot up heroin regularly but could stop at will for weeks or more at a time. I knew on the other hand skin-poppers (those who shot up under the skin rather than in a vein) and snorters who were completely addicted. I knew the highly dependent and the unable-to-stop, and within the latter category there were escalating people and steady-state people, like a boy we called Sudsy Pete the Junkie, who drank one six-pack of beer per day and always shot up the same amount of heroin. I knew people who switched around among drugs and were happy with any high and others who had to have one thing. As I say, we were young—in the group that I hung with, ages went from fourteen to the upper twenties. No doubt habits and their language evolved as folks grew older and their bodies' needs grew more urgent.

But the language of addiction still troubles me, and I don't know how to define myself. It is one flat term for an endless number of states of being, an attempt to name something at a molecular level, when living with drugs is more quantum, more a sea of probabilities. When I used heroin, I mostly snorted. I stopped using drugs after an overdose of methadone that my boyfriend, soon to be ex, slipped into an orange soda and gave to me as a kind of a joke (we called this "dosing" someone). I was desperately, crawl-on-the-floor-to-the-toilet, sick for a week, then somehow my body was empty, still wanting but also light, able to be done with the whole mess. I might still want to get high but I didn't need to. I assume somewhere in that illness was not just the methadone but my body purging its needs.

ADVERTISING

Mark wrote the ad we ran to sell the shore property. Which it would take several years for anyone to want. But at that time my mother was lost in the vague redundant world of her Alzheimer's; she never knew the loss happened. Melinda was dead; Mark's wife Beth was dead; many of the uncles and aunts—Kathleen, like Katherine, the first one to die, Joe, Bill, Mildred. Chris and I had scattered out of the Northeast long before.

And after Sandy nothing about that land was the same. The barrier islands that stood between us and the Atlantic, eaten away by warming, crumbled off acres of their protection in the hurricane. The beach, small as it was, was now half underwater, and would remain so. Water came up to the top of the bulkhead at the end of the street. When Chris and I went down to explore, on a calm May morning, waves slapped themselves onto the road. Entire streets near us were wiped out. Many houses stood whole from the front, ripped open in the back, like homes on a movie set.

Due to the water level and the likelihood of this happening again, the rules the family got for rebuilding required efforts at protection—stilts and boards that could withstand great pressure—not a quick-improvised chattel house.

Mark wrote the ad to sell the space and he began, *THIS ONCE GREAT BUNGALOW THAT WAS A TREASURE IN THE FAMILY WAS RAVISHED BY SANDY..

The capitals, and the two periods, are his. Mark is a high school teacher; he knows the difference between "ravaged" and "ravished."

OWNERS ARE ENTERTAINING ALL OFFERS! CALL NOW TO GET YOUR SLICE OF HEAVEN ON EARTH!

HEAVEN ON EARTH

We finally found a buyer willing to pay sixty thousand dollars for the shoreland. It took years. My grandfather had acquired—or taken it—seventy-one years before, for forty dollars, or four hundred dollars, or for nothing. I have heard all three versions of that story, and there's no one left living who would know. At the last minute my brother and my cousin Diana put together an offer to buy. Diana is building; my brother just put in his share to keep the property in the family, though he can use the new house occasionally if he wants. Diana has design plans for the new house, from a real architect. It is not a structure that could be called in any way a cottage or a bungalow. Two stories, a balcony from the second floor, leaning out at the bay. The changes are wrong from a family standpoint. For example, when you're above the earth, looking outward, you must be lying on the roof. That was how we did it and we had to look upward, at the stars and planets and constellations, rather than down.

Chris doesn't think he'll use the new place, but wants to know that he can.

SIX WINGS, FOUR FACES, MANY WOMEN

How many people have I told about the Summer Land who found it a great failure of the imagination? The rivers, the lakes. The mountains, the houses. The fact that you will still look pretty much like yourself, only, according to Davis, smaller, and glowy. I myself find the still-getting-older (slowly) theory of the Summer Land a step too far. Although perhaps it's a reconciliation to remaining in the body, paying the price of defying time by having a toe in it still.

Can't you give us in our paradise, people seem to say, something new?

We will have died and broken with all we have of physical existence. The hundred billion neurons in the brain will have ceased firing. The switchboard closes. People could break every bone in both of your feet and your nerve endings would be just fine with that.

In fact, the business of the nerves and the rest will have become decay, not just ceasing to pass messages but passively disassembling. I remember the death of my mother, the way I bought a plane ticket in the middle of the night and flew to the East Coast eight or nine hours after she died and my brother rushed me from Newark Airport to the funeral home to see my mother's body. She'd been dead barely a day at that point but the funeral home had to stay open until nine so I could "view" her.

My mother had chosen cremation and wasn't embalmed. Because of this, the nice woman at the funeral home said, I had to view her that evening or I could never view her at all. Viewing the body of a person who's died seemed imperative to everyone, and so I prayed that my plane not be delayed and I rushed.

If I'd waited any longer my mother would have decayed too much, nobody said to me then, nor to anyone else, nor would they ever. The euphemistic *you have this much time* that pushed me onto that plane and flung me out as fast as I could elbow by the first-class passengers had been clear.

As it was, my mother was both undeniably herself and undeniably not: Her lips had sunk and the skin of her cheeks clutched the bone, all her skin white and gone to wax, almost like the newborn's vernix. And the temperature. She was cold, like a stone you'd pick up on a beach, due I guess to the need to keep her refrigerated when people were not there to *view* her. When you encounter a person as a corpse it's hard not to be stunned by the memory of all this body accomplished while living: yawning and rolling as it wakes from sleep, reaching a hand into a mailbox, tapping its big toe, all while managing not to decay. Remarkable, yet the least of people can do this.

I put my hand on my mother's forehead—something I'd rarely done in life—and took it away.

Given that death makes us so strange so instantly, how can we accept the familiarity of the Summer Land as the next world? AJ Davis fought in the Civil War, notably in the Battle of Fort Donelson, where he describes seeing a man shot so that his brains flew all over the countryside (while the man's new spiritual self hovered overhead). Davis knew the frailty of the human body. Putting all of us back in ours in the Summer Land took a chutzpah or a faith, or both of these, mingled.

And while many people I know laugh at the Summer Land, the sameness of the Summer Land, not even the most conventional Christians seem too behind the angels and heavenly choirs and the orderly ranks of the blessed that's the traditional view of heaven. It all feels too much like a high school glee club. In fact, I think all these folks (Davis would call these traditionalists *religionists*) spend so much time getting lost in the mathematics—six wings on the seraphim above the throne, four faces on the cherubim beside the throne, seventy-two virgins in paradise—because they don't want to admit it all sounds not just improbable but dull.

Paradise is hard, I'm saying. We want something we can't imagine but then we want to be able to imagine it. What do we want, other than to have this life without any of its flaws? We want the Summer Land.

SUCH A THING

Smithereens is not death. Death is not smithereens.

Smithereens partakes of fission. An atomy rupture. Perhaps it's where the quantum world breaks into the large. It could have to do with ravishment, though it would be ravishment by a strange god leaving you full of a creature not-of-your-flesh. You would be the woman wombing the giant egg. The birth of which may harm you.

When a thing disappears in such a way that multitudes go with it, that is smithereens. When you can't write it an epitaph because it took with itself out of existence the language that could hold it, that is smithereens. It may be that smithereens violates the principle of the conservation of mass.

The word comes from the Irish *smidirin,* a small blown fragment, but there is no singular form for the word it engendered, smithereens.

Of course, things need smithereens sometimes, or there would be no new things.

SMITHEREEN

She would tilt her face up to me.

And close her eyes. Like a cup brimming, steadying its restless surface. She didn't easily give any part of herself to anyone else. My husband and I called her a *noli me tangere,* someone unwilling to be touched.

Her head tilted the same way laying out at the funeral home before they shipped her to the crematorium. When did I cry? Only when I learned the fire did not burn her all to ash but to bone, bones then ground in a human-grade grinder.

When my mother tilted her face to me I had my things, my colors, my brushes, laid out. We would probably be in the bathroom, her seated on the closed toilet. I started with the lips. Once the lips had color, the architecture of the face showed itself, and other shades came into focus.

My mother had the same eye shape as me. We share the deep-lidded and very round orbits with wisps of brow, though my eyes are dark brown and hers, hazel. Or that was her word for them. Like all eyes of that color hers had flecks of many shades and could look different colors, depending. If I chose green eye shadow it drew out specks of leaf. Blue, a gray-blue like flint. I suppose in my way I chose the shade of mother I wanted and filled her in.

I had gotten skilled with makeup. In middle school my friend Alice and I stole it from local five-and-dime stores almost daily, and finally had to hitchhike to other towns to do what we called our "hocking." No store near us would let us in. In my mid-teens I sold Avon for drug money for a few months, and I got samples. I followed drawings of faces and eyes and learned where to put the light colors and where to put the dark, the highlights, the shadows. As I say, I got good at this. My mother was helpless with anything beyond lipstick in a tube.

I can't recall when I first did her makeup—I know then it was my idea, for some occasion, like a wedding—but after that she would ask me, if she went out somewhere. She had a wonderful bone structure and looked striking with just a little help. Or makeup made her more obviously pretty, in a way that surprised her that first time, then pleased her after. And since I would not otherwise have been welcome to touch her, that made the whole thing feel solemn to me, like a worshipper who pours over Shiva the milk and butter on one holy day every year, the only time he gets to approach.

On the table at the funeral home, my mother lay with her eyes shut, her face tilted up. Her hair was wrong, pushed back into a roll from her forehead, and she wore thick black glasses I'd never seen before. Through these strangenesses, that old bathroom pose of relinquishment and expectation. I can't remember now if I thought at the funeral home about putting makeup on her face, or if I thought of it afterward. Somehow it came into my mind, and it has never left, how I could have pulled out the small bag of products I carry in my purse.

Coral on the lips, a pinker gloss. A light streak under the brow.
Medium brown on the brow-wisps. Dark shadow brushed
along the back of those eyes, to give a beautiful depth, if only
they could open. A dust of blue along the lid. Blush. A foundation of Bare Naturale powdered mineral.

NOT THERE

My mother died at ninety-four, six weeks after coming down
with a urinary tract infection. That initial infection, diagnosed
as minor, led to a Boschian period in which my mother was
checked into the hospital for an overnight stay to get stronger
antibiotics, then deteriorated so quickly she never came home.
It was a long and painful process during which she eked away
even though she was, literally, belted to the earth.

The Boschian quality came largely from the hospital itself,
and I think Mary Baker Eddy, a woman who relished being
right above all things, would have taken satisfaction in her
apostate being driven batshit crazy by medical care.

Back and forth my mother went: hospital, discharge to
Alzheimer's ward, hospital again, discharge to the hospice
we'd been begging for, thank God, finally. She was in her sixth
year of Alzheimer's, a disease that had also claimed my grandmother. In spite of her weakness, my mother had become an
impossibly restless body. She rolled, she swung her legs from
one side of the hospital bed to the other, she flailed her arms.
As she readied to exit this life, she became pure force, and the
nurses had to tie her with a thick belt to the bed. That belt
looked overwhelming on my tiny mother—four-foot-ten and
maybe ninety pounds at the time.

My mother's confinement enraged her and her body
worked like a thing possessed. She reminded me of the souls
in the Middle Ages who danced the tarantella to exhaustion

because they thought it would cure a dangerous spider bite: She did not seem as if she wanted to move so much as that she had to. My mother, who no longer had a clear understanding of her life, wanted to live. In that drive she wore herself down, and her body seemed on the verge of flying off into its constituent parts—the primal molecules, the fissioning stardust, the supernova spitting its carbon.

"You are useless!" she screamed at us: my brother, my father, and me. She moaned *Take me home, take me home* for hours in a high, possessed voice, then snapped at me, "Take me home, you're my daughter and you have to do what I tell you," her face taking on those lines of my grandmother's face, that look that tries to brook no opposition but in my mother's case, only underlined its failure. She cursed me with the fate of ending up in a hospital, strapped down, like her, at the end of my life. She yelled this at me—*Don't smile, Susanne, you have my genes, you're going to end up just like me*—then looked off, abstractedly, the rage draining off her face like something physical. She turned back and looked at my feet.

"I really like your shoes, Susanne," she said. "Where'd you get those shoes?"

This was how it was. She vowed never to forgive with the fury of a Lear, then noticed our shoes.

We showed her hundreds of photographs—my son, my cat and dog, my garden, boats—to try to distract her. We gave her a date for each one: *This is Jin back in 2000, the dog two months ago, in the daylilies.* She never stayed distracted for long. In her anger and her frenzy my mother threw punches at people and scratched them, both nurses and aides and her family. She turned her nails against herself. When my mother died she had a face scratched by her own hand and a black eye no one in the Alzheimer's facility had been able to explain to us. My husband and I guessed someone she hit had hit her back.

She went blind in one eye and the skin on that side of her face loosened and drooped; she became a wax figure candled on one side. This began right before her first hospitalization, and her new blindness proved a condition I could not get any doctor to take seriously, which wasn't surprising, since in the hospital we dealt with a new doctor each day and each one's notes always seemed too inscrutable or inadequate for the next one. At times one doctor would look at the prior doctor's diagnosis and snort.

My mother cried *I can't see* in that possessed voice. I would direct the doctor of the day—who tended to flit in and out with no warning, staying only minutes, so we learned to stand watch for him, her, or them, not even going to the bathroom if a doctor was rumored to be on the floor—to the eye, and the doctor would say, "But didn't she come in that way?" fumbling through the inscrutable notes. I'd say no and the whole eye thing would start again. Most likely it was caused by lung cancer—a related condition called Horner's Syndrome—and not by a stroke. Two doctors agreed with that explanation and two disagreed, and that seemed as much certainty as I would ever get.

"I want to get out of here!" my mother shrieked over and over from her bed.

"I just came in the hospital to visit someone," she started saying after a couple of days. "Why did you make me stay?"

She could never quite remember who she'd come to visit, but she was convinced of the truth of her story, as she believed we put her in and could get her out. She could not understand why we, from her point of view, ignored the facts and her needs. She cried to go the bathroom, as she could never remember she'd just gone. We let her go every ten minutes—it took two nurses to get her into and onto the toilet so it was never a popular request, but the staff soon realized we too could be unrelenting. In between we had to say no, though she hollered nonstop *Take me home* and *I have to go to the bathroom and you have to let me* and *You're useless* again.

People tell me the woman who railed at me through the last weeks of her life was not my mother, not really. It was her disease talking, they'd say; she had succumbed to the Alzheimer's, an alien force. *It wasn't her.* As if she'd disassembled already. Though I recognized my mother's anger as herself, pure—she had gone raw and deep, beyond and below her filters. As she lost her fiancé in the Second World War, she had been that person. As she gave up her job and stayed home with us children, she had been that person. As she read to me from her scuffed volumes of *Mother Goose* and the Brothers Grimm and the stories I begged for terrified me and kept me awake, she had been that person. As her own mother left her four children again and again, only for my mother's two to cling to her in the kitchen of our apartment, she had been this: restrained. Angry. As Rilke put it of the Chamberlain's death in *The Notebooks of Malte Laurids Brigge,* my mother died her own hard death, one she had carried her whole life long inside her.

ENDURE

During my mother's last weeks we spent most of the day at the hospital, in a blitz of medical language. And my father ran it all through his malaprop translator and came out with his own terms: The group of affiliated physicians she saw was called AMD, but he called them the *ATMs.* Her urinary tract infection morphed into her *urinal,* her intravenous tube (IV) became her *HIV.* Ensure, which she continued to drink at the hospital, he called (heartbreakingly) *Endure.* And so on. It's truer I think to say he took these words and rolled them around in his head till they stuck to something that helped him remember, and maybe gave added sense. She was dying with the certainty of HIV in its early days, doctors withdrew our cash with abandon, and she lost weight by the day, her Ensure keeping her barely in flesh.

Still, as we rarely had more than five minutes with a doctor, and that not daily, I had to interrupt my father when doctors came and rephrase the questions that came out as things like *Why did his wife still have the HIV? Was the urinal better? Where were the other ATMs?* My father irritated some doctors and shut down others who tried to puzzle him out, but in his worry and his pride he wanted to be the one who spoke to the doctors on behalf of his dying wife. *She has a urinary tract infection,* they'd say, or just *What are you saying?* I'd say, *He means we thought the IV would come out yesterday,* and my father would say, *The HIV.* He got angry at me for butting in. I tried to give the doctors hand signals to ignore him and listen to me but that never worked.

If I could have met with them alone, I would have said, *Don't you see, he has had to create a language for this. You have yours.*

WHAT SHE CARRIED

My grandmother too carried that ruptured seed inside her, that hard death. I couldn't have predicted it, given that she did not believe in death, just considering it a step that removes you from your illusion of a body and leaves your spirit the same. But her death was, if anything, harder than my mother's, and she finally asked to see doctors. Worse than anything, she returned to some earlier incarnation of herself: She was afraid.

PLANET ZOMBIE

I stop by my grandmother's house a lot at this time of her deterioration and death, the 1980s. I live in New York, in Brooklyn, not today's Brooklyn but my father's cheap and crime-ridden Brooklyn, and I'm newly married. I come when I can. I find even in the heat she's shut and thumb locked her windows; she will crash across the room, decrepit as she is, to slam a window or a door. *Demons have been coming in,* my mother says wearily.

These things my grandmother does get categorized by my mother as *shenanigans.* May chases the demons through the windows and locks them out. This is a shenanigan (though, as with *smithereens,* I'm not sure there exists a singular). I see my grandmother's fear but don't ask her to describe the demons. I am young, in my twenties, too shortsighted to realize how I will someday want to know. Is it Simon puffing in and out those windows? Is it Louis? Men from the First World War, they and their gassed and severed limbs, together maybe? Apart maybe?

For the last few years of my grandmother's life, when I ask my mother how her mother's doing, she invariably says, *She's failing.* As if her mother takes a daily test on remaining alive, and she flunks it.

Many things are now terrifying to my grandmother, including the home aides my mother and her siblings have been sending to help. May runs them out of the house, quite literally, giving chase and slamming the door. Her hair stands up, her clothes smell pee-ish and their folds scatter crumbs. She's filthy, far less than she ought to be.

She lives in the primal stew of fears like my childhood fears, her own spirits turned against her. Death is not an awful thing, but this is.

My grandfather long gone, my grandmother till now the happiest person left living alone I have ever met. At seventy-nine she treks through Kenya, at eighty-one she goes to England, and at eighty-six she forgets her cat needs food and water. The tea water boils out of the kettle, scorching the bottom. Her children, other than Mildred—who remains a sympathetic child but rarely helps—vie with one another to be hardboiled about her.

"Bung her into a nursing home," says my uncle.

"If she falls down the stairs, she falls down the stairs," says my mother to me. "I'm sick and tired of her shenanigans."

That's my mother, not only tired of the shenanigans, but sick with them. She's never one without the other. I have myself made her plenty sick as well as tired over the years. And someday her shenanigans will yield the same result with me, but she doesn't know that.

I find myself wishing the siblings would fake their devotion a little better, but I understand. Their mother chose travel over them, Christian Science over them, her life and its pleasures and purposes over them. Now she is saying: *Wait a minute. Find me doctors and nurses. Come take care of me.* And *Help me not to be afraid.* And their point is: too late.

BLIZZACANE, S'NOREASTERCANE, FRANKENSTORM

Hurricane Sandy made landfall in New Jersey under a full moon, which raised the tides, and so the storm surge, by some twenty percent. A full moon over our bay was an amazing thing to see—large, rugged, yet almost palpating with a warm, yellowish light, the color of light from a candle. It felt both impossibly close and impossibly distant and often had dark vein-thin clouds scuffing its surface. We would go out to watch it though we often pretended to be predicting the weather, red-sky-at-nighting, reading the whitecaps running like pale rabbits on the waves. A moon like that was one of the only fully romantic things I remember about the shore, and I imagine the moments before the surge struck, it and the rearing water looked very beautiful.

Sandy began life as a tropical cyclone, hitting land in the Caribbean and then working its way up to make landfall again at the New Jersey shore. It—or she—followed the path of my grandfather. Like my grandfather, British by his Barbados birth and then Canadian and then American, Sandy changed its colors. From a cyclone it became a hurricane but lost its central eye as it approached New Jersey, running at that time straight into a winter storm. This storm wrapped itself around the tropical core, creating both warm and cold fronts. Sandy generated massive flooding, steaming rain, freezing winds, and snow. All these occurrences were wildly unprecedented. As the *Washington Post* put it, the only natural disaster lacking in Sandy was "a plague of locusts."

Sandy, like most hybrid storms, spread out over a great area—it impacted twenty-four states and its northern incarnation was the size of nine of the tropical Sandys. Sandy was never one thing, after reaching my home state, and for this reason has had many names: Hurricane Sandy, Superstorm Sandy, and the portmanteau names in my title.

Sandy hit land at Seaside Heights on the Atlantic and about seven miles from our bungalows. Seaside's a cheesy town with a tacky boardwalk, a Ferris wheel I wheeled on for many hours when young, tripping on acid. Sandy was a milestone storm in its damage, physical and monetary, the most expensive in US history at that time—twenty billion dollars in direct damage and roughly the same amount in lost business. Sandy's loss of life is not exact but probably stood at around two hundred fifty. The storm would still be unprecedented and talked about if it weren't for the many freakish weather events happening now, each more and more powerful.

I saw photos after of a gutted Holly Park with crude signs and graffiti that read *Holly Park Strong*. Listing a place name and the word *Strong* after a disaster has become something people do, though I remember seeing this and rebelling from the sentiment. The words mean the people of this place are strong, they'll get through and get back to where they were before, though of course they can't and they don't. We have been New Orleans Strong, Orlando Strong, Boston Strong. What I ask is permission to be weak.

Sandy happened in late October of 2012. My parents, my mom barely getting around with a walker, spent the week without heat or electricity as it hit the north of the state. My brother stayed with them and they heated the house with the gas jets on their stove. They could have taken shelter, for free, at an assisted living place a half mile from their house. They insisted on home, keeping all four burners turned up, and wandering through the house muffled in sweaters and bathrobes. I did not think about the shore bungalows at all until I knew my parents had their power back.

At this point, though, I often need to tickle memories when I explain Sandy and the loss of the bungalows to people here. They say *I remember that storm but remind me.* We've had wildfires eating California, north and south, we've had Hurricane Harvey with its almost two hundred billion worth of damage, coming in a year, 2017, that saw ten hurricanes and six major hurricanes hit the Atlantic. Names of hurricanes are dropped from the name roster if there's considerable loss of life. 2017 retired Harvey, Nate, Irma, and Maria.

There's some dispute among climate scientists about whether warming makes storms more frequent. There's no dispute about the relationship between warming caused by carbon emissions and a storm's severity and breadth. The melting ice caps have caused the seas to rise, and warming has made their surfaces hotter (and cyclones to happen later and later in the year, so Sandy's joining forces with northern bad weather was bizarre then but likely to become common). Cyclones and hurricanes suck energy from the warmth of the ocean, and the high seas make storm surges much higher. And we have much more moisture in our atmosphere than we should— each degree Fahrenheit our temperature rises puts four percent more moisture in the air. This damp feeds rainfall and floods.

I understand our memory fatigue. We've had so many freak storms.

The carbon in the universe comes from fusion within dying stars. Carbon is necessary for any kind of life as we understand it, and the time it took to make these stars and have them die to make our carbon is so immense that it makes the need for consciousness in the universe that much more unlikely. Carbon, from the point of view of our bodies and our planet, is very precious. But now, sad to say, also lethal. It set the cosmos ticking toward us and now us ticking away from it.

HOW TO DIE KNOWING
THAT YOU'LL LIVE FOREVER

In spite of time's unreality, the body we have (like my mother's body) has what we call a *span* of time. We live in an elaborate contraption with gears meshing toward failure, even if assault on the permeable stuff like heart and lung and brain does not get you before the whole runs out. The basic bits of what you are will always exist; in this form you wear now, though, it's a web of vulnerabilities and drives toward close. Your cells are created with a limited number of times they can divide, and each division shortens those chromosomal telomeres, rendering your new cells more unstable.

Your cells do not work alone: Hundreds of internal processes coincide to wear you down. A process called glycation releases damaging free radicals. Things like the sun, which we need, begin to damage. It is elaborate and choreographed.

Life in a body, in the proverbial *meat suit,* is one of those fables or fairy tales of the bad bargain, the fate someone lashes out against and so causes to be. The king learns his son will kill him so he casts him out, and then the son, not recognizing his father because he's never met him, does in fact kill him.

Your parents—or one of them at least—may have loved you, but they put you into this body. Out of love for you, they signed a contract with your end. They are their own wicked queens, their own horned Maleficents. You can step out of time by existing as your simplest parts, your protons and electrons, your charm quarks and up quarks. But you don't. You accept that carbonating assembly, that consciousness, so you can count your way down to its close: the fingerprick on the spindle, the return of the wicked queen.

And so as I wish my mother back into her body I wish her back into time, which is to say back to the meat suit, starting her way out again. Bearing the turtle shell on her back, swallowing again the seed of her death. And surely before birth, something—angel or ogre or trench-coat Morpheus from *The Matrix*—offers us that choice: Swallow this and accept the fallacy called time. Perhaps my mother now argues fiercely against doing so, against my yearning. And my grandmother May, as I think of her and evoke her. My observation may cause them in some way to exist. I disturb them, shape them, when all they want is to keep fizzing in the everything-at-once. It may be the true heaven. The life in which perhaps smithereens and the Summer Land are one.

It may not help that I mostly want my mother here to tell her today I planted twelve wild strawberry plants I ordered online, and each was amazingly tiny, like a thread. It took three leaves to cover my thumbnail. I have no faith something that little could survive, but no doubt my mother felt that way at some point about me.

I want to send her pictures of the irises, which for some reason decided to bloom (dozens) this year, instead of what they've been doing, sending up only their bladelike leaves. All are purple. Right now everything in the garden's purple, blue, or white—the blue scilla, the white rhododendrons and Solomon's seal, the white lilac and the lilac lilac. I am trying to dig in some bleeding hearts, for variety. She would appreciate all this.

How do you die into this life beyond space-time? You learn to feel yourself going, every second, every nanosecond, some scurf blown from your skin, some cells expelled with a breath, all holding that form a while, sooner or later tumbling apart. Know that you are a "quark blob," as Max Tegmark puts it. As you are a quark blob, you live. As you are a quark blob assembled into a human, you do not stay alive, but you do get to narrate this artificially limited chunk of timelessness to yourself. Think of the supernovas; know that your ends have always been spectacular. You can say goodbye to some of your ten-to-the-twenty-ninth-power quarks and electrons. You can say, with medieval poet Guido Cavalcanti—himself long gone, now rolling somewhere in a black hole or a supernova— *Because I cannot hope to return again, go on by yourself, little poems.*

You can say, *Donna me prega.* Because a woman asks me.

PART V

REMAINS

REMAINS

What's left of humans, or any creature. We call them this though the "remains" may constitute all of a person that physically existed, so the implication of "remains" as "what's left" applies not literally but to something inscrutable. The cells' abilities to divide. Consciousness, the neurons' chatty gab. Phi, which at least must break down into small minor phi. What in my consciousness has not shut its doors. That part of my mother that had almost extinguished in life, though what remained of her after death still bore no resemblance to that denatured her of the last years.

It can mean what we put into the ground, and do not remove again. Actually this latter is a lie: We dig up graves all the time, to add more bodies, to build highways, though collectively we pretend we don't. I will not be remains, but I will have them. *Susanne's remains,* people will say, attributing them to me, though there will be no *me* to possess them. And I've asked that they be burned.

NEW THINGS

Unlike my mother with her mother, I found a tenderness with my mother in those last years. Her lost memory proved a blessing for the two of us. Until the weeks of her dying, she had few demons, or fewer than she'd had in the past. Once even a simple thing like my cooking for my parents would draw her self-doubts, though cooking was a thing she often asked me to do.

"This is good," she'd say, and then, looking at my father, "You think it's better than mine," or "I guess she's more of a gourmet cook than me." After her Alzheimer's she would eat with real pleasure, though I never made anything fancy, just things like meatloaf and roast chicken. Whatever, she'd eat a few mouthfuls with interest and the clacking chew her dentures caused, and look around the table and say, smiling, "Hire the cook!" She laughed shyly, pleased with herself. She grew tinier in old age, and ate sitting on a cushion, and I can still see her face looking up at us. When we laughed back she'd say it again, "Hire the cook!" forgetting how many meals she'd already punctuated with that joke.

My food was no longer part of a pattern of food. This was true of other things as well; my teaching job, my son and his attachment to me. Things just were what they were, existing in the moment, isolated from the context provided by memory. She had gone Buddhistic and had only the now.

I helped her to the bathroom and sometimes helped her in it, helped her dress, and rubbed lotion on her hands. I carried her diapers—she called them her *drawers*—when we went out together, while she still could go out. We went to a restaurant she and my father liked, a few blocks from their house. I helped her to the restroom there and handed her her *drawers* under the stall door. Perhaps if I had done any of these things, in her mind, repetitively, it would have been too much—she would have felt beholden, weak. But all of this happened over and over again precisely once.

THE SMILE FADES

In the middle of this more tender time with her Alzheimer's, my mother began erasing me from her memories. It may be that the me she remembered and the me she knew now were irreconcilable, and she needed to blot one out.

She first erased me from the trip we took together to meet my father's family in Italy. I was in my early twenties at the time. I got sick on the return flight, throwing up, then lying nauseated across a few seats on the plane.

My father showed her a photo we had taken of his town, Gesualdo. We showed her photos then and told stories that went with them, to help her remember. She sat in her spot on the gold floral couch, the cat pillow she used to stare at under one arm, the glass of milk she poured and drank from sporadically all day in front of her. I always tried to take that milk away, assuming it grew bacteria in the overheated room. She never let me.

"Chris was so sick then," she told my father.

He said, "Not Chris, that was Susanne," and my mother, who'd also gone deaf, said, "You're right, isn't it funny Susanne wasn't there. Where was she? Why wouldn't she go on a trip like that?"

I said, "But I was there," and my mother just repeated, "Where did Susanne go?"

This became a pattern, with my brother doing the things he did, like playing Little League games, and also the things I did, like working in the stands so I could be stuck somewhere during Little League games, though often the two activities were not compatible. When I visited my mother during this time, if she did not sit directly in front of me, she would keep saying I was gone. I would hear her clomping her walker from the bathroom: "Susanne's left for the airport. Susanne's not here anymore."

And my mother would hear any contradiction of her version of our earlier history as the question of where I was at that time, an inquiry she met with wonder: "You're right, where was Susanne? What was she doing?" She seemed not unhappy I was gone so much, but puzzled by it. She never seemed to take it personally, feel that she'd lost me again and again. She seemed, mother of the Cheshire cat, struck by these new memories' revealing an aspect of her life she hadn't previously noticed, my chronic disappearance.

APPARENTLY I AM HIDING
IN MY MOTHER'S ROOM

Are you there?

It's the voice my mother used when I tucked myself knee-to-chin in my parents' room at night, a child in Elizabeth, hunched lump by the door: riding out the hard gallop of a nightmare. Or fear-soaked and unable to sleep. (*No I'm nowhere.*) The ghosts from the cemetery across the street from our apartment, the ones my brother said only eat little girls. The wood creak, the man cupping the knife, he who can pass among us because he wears a good hat.

I am forbidden to wake my parents up. Or that's what I remember. I was often afraid at night, and maybe had just exhausted their patience.

Are you there?

My mother's voice, sleep-croaky. She hears steps but doesn't assume it's a ghost or a homicidal middle-aged man, only one of her children, and at that, the girl. Whose daytime manic energy yields to panic in the dark.

I wonder, if you give birth to your child, when you realize the molecular link between you really is severed, when you accept that you can't fold them back in. You can't access a single one of this child's molecules any longer. You can't even convince her she won't die tonight. You can just chase her out of your room.

Are you there?
I ask this of my mother now, ground bone, quantum waves that become particles if I attend to them. *She'll stay alive in our hearts* maybe has its truth, if the heart can be a quantum watchman. How funny, I say, observing (wave slides into particle), how everything falls suddenly blue and purple and white here in the garden. The wild strawberries, dug in, have pretty much disappeared. Threads, threads with fruit.

If only I'd been born knowing what I know now. I was never fair to my mother, perhaps, this woman like all of us Jenga-ed into time, piled to the great collapse.

Are you there?
The hospital always had a woman orderly sit in a folding chair in my mother's room to watch her, in light of her escape attempts. Sometimes this woman left when we arrived, often not. There were at least a dozen separate women in this role and I can't remember anything about them besides that they stared at their hands or thumbed a phone, ungodly bored. Their work could be relieved by the time reaching a certain o'clock and a replacement watcher slipping in, or it could be relieved by my mother's death. Either way the watching had been done.

Are you there?

This is my mother, calling out to the universe from her deathbed: *Don't stop looking away now.*

MY MOTHER, MY GRANDMOTHER, AND ME IN HEAVEN, KNOWN AS THE SUMMER LAND (A PROLEPTIC)

Though she has worn us, slept wrapped in our leavings, cut us with scissors from the stem, she evades. We have none of the novelty of a Davis or a Blavatsky. My mother and I see flickers now and then through the bushes; fingerlights. There's hurrying and there's fluttering. My grandmother, small then and smaller now, moves continually away, like a repulsed magnetic force. Her form lobs itself into the bushes I remind myself come partly from my son and husband, partly from other people I've loved. And partly from those I've disliked, with the pointless over-intensity with which I dislike people: for wearing those knit beanie caps with the side strings. For being the man who asks me if I'm going to "win today," who has a wispy man-bun. If I can kill myself here in the Summer Land, surely I can remain petty. Though I acknowledge these folks too rain down (or up?) on me, forming themselves into the trappings of my life here.

My mother will be somewhat lonely, I'd guess, here in the Summer Land. She is not gregarious. We, her family, smother her with our emanations. My death would even have lessened the substance of her new world, in some subtle way. My mother now may be glad enough to see me.

Would she invite me into her new home? Perhaps there's no going that far. She might want to catch up, hear what's going on with my garden and my cat. There too my presence might soon erase itself.

All three of us drawn to the edge of the water. It feels like what we left, maybe like our joint home at Holly Park, though our climate in the Summer Land cannot tug and baffle this water as it did on earth.

I could imagine my grandmother being resentful of what happened to her bungalows, though my mother and I alone couldn't halt the production of carbon. Still. She tended to hold people responsible for things. There might be a tug between her desire to avoid us and her desire to scold: *I left things so pretty for you.*

QUESTION: WHAT IS THE SCIENTIFIC STATEMENT OF BEING?

THERE IS NO LIFE, TRUTH, INTELLIGENCE, NOR SUBSTANCE IN MATTER.
—From *Science and Health with Key to the Scriptures,* by Mary Baker Eddy

My mother in her hospital room couldn't bear to be alone. She'd yell that my brother and my father and I wanted her to die and we'd leave, but then she'd beg us to come back. And we did. She rarely recalled what she'd said to offend us. My brother and I took turns being in New Jersey during the six weeks of her death. Whichever of us was there held one hand of hers, and my father held the other. She stretched out her hands to us as we approached. She forgot being a *noli me tangere.* Her memory faltered more, but what she did remember didn't include a blank space, like a badly doctored photograph, where I'd once been.

Because of her extreme agitation she had to be drugged, with many of the drugs I'd been given when I was young: Haldol, Thorazine, the major antipsychotics. And often I was the one going to ask the nurses to give her a dose, or an extra dose, when she became impossible to deal with, as she gave permission for me to be drugged like this in the past, during those shock treatment years. I became her, or we became some kind of composite of ourselves, entangled. I made terrible decisions about her consciousness, but I didn't know any other decisions I could make. And for once in our lives I could tell what she was feeling more intimately than anybody in the room.

The nurses would come in with their paper cups and my mother would swallow, then lie there murky, rolling in and out of sleep, calling *Susanne? Susanne?* her voice in its fear catching. *I'm here,* I said, *Yes. I'm here. I'm here I'm here.*

THE BINDING PROBLEM, AGAIN

I wished for my mother to die. As wishes can, this one had an almost physical growth, from a tiny darting thing when her hospital days dragged, to a heaviness as tied to my body as she was to her bed. It jerked me awake at night. That anyone in my place would have felt the same, that no doubt my father and brother were feeling the same, that my mother did truly suffer, formed good reasons that nevertheless didn't help. If this could happen with us then it could happen with me, my son and husband could wish this. Any of us could be lost in such a way that the emptiness seems soothing. Even the last disposals looked forward to, the nylons and nighties and old girdles thrown in bags, peeling back the human layers that no longer have a center.

I have to remind myself of other things. That my mother and I lived to trade places. And that she died fed and clean and with family who wouldn't leave her, unlike her own mother. If my mother could have understood her death, seen the pieces of it from the outside with her mind intact, she would have in a strange way liked it.

AN ENDLESS FEEDBACK LOOP

I have told you about my garden but not our house, the Big Bungalow I could call it, by my father's reckoning of the studio as the Little, built well over a century ago by a doctor who tended patients housed in an asylum for syphilitics behind us. Or so I've been told by a neighborhood historian. A small house, a refuge from that place, perhaps a sign of the doctor's maturing income. Many psychiatrists then lived with their patients. I heard this doctor's patients lingered in the end stages, bacterial spirochetes like tiny ramen noodles in the brain.

Neurosyphilis can look like bipolar disorder—shifting moods, grandeur, delusions.

This fact of the madhouse I have from local historians. That place became a Montessori school, then a private home. It's still there. My doctor did what he could in the era before antibiotics and drugs like Haldol. Psychiatrists—often called alienists then—used baths, spinning chairs that spun patients to a dizzied flop, emetics and laxatives to treat them. At the end of the day the doctor tied down the frantic ones and walked the thirty feet to his house, likely eating a dinner of halibut or salmon, maybe mussels chipped off the docks down the street. He'd sit in his narrow living room, with piles of medical journals, reading about new treatments like music (best if patients formed their own bands; could his?) and research on the type of cranium that lent itself to madness. Too, he holds research about cranial weight and insanity, and he tests these theories himself when a patient dies; he measures the skull by how it displaces seawater in a small tank, keeping notes. And he studies the bumps in the cranium and patterns in the grooves of

238 of course his modern medicine was all wrong in this.

the brain, signs his modern medicine considered key indicators of madness (that bulge of Destructiveness behind the ear), though of course his modern medicine was all wrong in this.

Evenings he sits where I sit, perhaps too with a cat at his shoulder. He considers what he does very new and caring, just as we think of our own medicine. If he ever tried to picture the woman who might now live in his house, his imagination wouldn't reach: a woman in pants who works and votes. A madwoman tugging at him, calm in his sanctuary, with her mind.

The window glass in this room dates back to the doctor's time, and though I know that time is in a cosmic sense likely to be false, the glass Friend the cat and I look through has done what it does over many years, and flowed to form wavelike patterns in the bottom. It gives the present of hunched maple and parked cars, looked at through its bends, a smear like the stuff of memory.

HERE BULLET II

I go back to my father's in May, to be there on the day that would have been his and my mother's anniversary. My room is the house's attic, and when my parents moved into this house, all my junk got stored in this space. There's a flimsy embossed box that I've had since I was a kid, and one day as I go through the room opening things in a trance of boredom, I look inside. There's a sand dollar, which I got on Cape Cod as a child. Then under the tissue the sand dollar rests on, I feel a small lump and find a bullet, small and several tones of copper. The bullet has been fired—it has striations—but it's pretty clean. I remember suddenly that I saved this bullet, which dates from when I was a teenager, so that I would remember the story of how I got it, a story that had importance to me, such that I

wanted to have moments throughout my life when I pushed
it back into my mind. I have no memory however of the story.

THERE

On the day that would have been my parents' anniversary,
May 9th, my father and I visit the place that my father calls
the *moosoleum,* stress on the *moo.* My mother's cremains rest
there, or clump in the humidity, or riffle with the tread of her
spirit. Who knows. The moosoleum is actually a normal graveyard called the Fairview, where behind some gravestones lies a
curved, reddish wall that holds squares with names and dates
(my mother's, 1920 to 2014), and behind them, niches for jars.

The Fairview rolls off as far as I can see, with long stretches
of grass flawless and sheened with chemicals, and a small lake
with fountains. I notice this time driving in that the place
resembles the Summer Land, in particular Davis's sketch of the
view at the edge of Lake Mornia. The largest of the lake's fountains looks like a big person under the surface is spitting the
water up, but doing it very, very well, arced water fast enough
to shift between drop and mist.

But the geese give it all away: We're on earth, and this slice
of it houses flocks of Canadian geese that honk, waddle, and
shit, so the lawn's dabbed with soft parti-colored shit tubes. My
father and I have to tie blue paper booties around our shoes to
walk the short distance to my mother's stone. I would just as
soon clean my shoes later, but my father's fastidious about his
clothing.

One of my fears about my death, apart from homicide,
is that it will be ludicrous. I tie the booties onto my ninety-
year-old father's shoes and then my own, and it is completely
ludicrous. We slide together across the grass, two oversized,
emancipated infants.

My mother died angry and confused, tormented and then torn from life as, from her perspective, she visited some imaginary friend in a hospital. I think of spiritualist logic about hauntings, feeling the hairlift of her maybe-presence flitting between us and the spat water. Perhaps she's why the geese caterwaul out of their long necks.

Or maybe this is her Summer Land and she loves it, or it's not but she's in the Summer Land anyway and not, if the afterlife is kind, too likely to stay in the path of her mother. I'm not there yet. I picture her looking for someone to talk to and running into my house's doctor, who has aggressive sideburns and tells her that in life he lived in Bellingham. Oh, she thinks (she would love to converse by thinking) my daughter lives there. *Where did you live?*

He tells her, and she says, *Funny, that sounds a lot like my daughter's house,* but the thought ends there.

SUPERPOSITION/STORM SURGE

I know the cottages are gone from Holly Park: They became real, and once they could be grasped by people outside the family—pinned to a numeral, to a street name, through the double-slit of the storm—they vanished. I'll never see them again. I could imagine my grandmother's return: She would come to my back door so she could pass the beds of roses and strawberries, raspberries and mint.

Perhaps May watched Hurricane Sandy from the Summer Land, the storm surge lashing through the back of our cottages. She excused herself from her tea table at the lake, dove to earth. She came in her small, lighted, and eternal body, in her bright clothes, though once here she'd choose to divest herself even of those clothings, jumping from the porch right into the sea.

I imagine this could be true. I imagine that in spite of her metaphysics my grandmother had grown too attached to the place to leave and stay gone. She's unlike my mother, safe in her ungreedy afterlife. May swims and will keep swimming to the blue table that the sea gulps and tongues up again with wild speed, bouncing it out of the yacht basin into the bay proper. In her new form she looks like those lights in the night water my cousin and I once combed through our fingers, the vague and popping gleams you could and couldn't touch. Perhaps in the chaos of time it was always her.

21st CENTURY ESSAYS
David Lazar and Patrick Madden, Series Editors

This series from Mad Creek Books is a vehicle to discover, publish, and promote some of the most daring, ingenious, and artistic nonfiction. This is the first and only major series that announces its focus on the essay—a genre whose plasticity, timelessness, popularity, and centrality to nonfiction writing make it especially important in the field of nonfiction literature. In addition to publishing the most interesting and innovative books of essays by American writers, the series publishes extraordinary international essayists and reprint works by neglected or forgotten essayists, voices that deserve to be heard, revived, and reprised. The series is a major addition to the possibilities of contemporary literary nonfiction, focusing on that central, frequently chimerical, and invariably supple form: The Essay.

---

*Annual Gournay Prize Winner